Floating Hogans
in
Monument Valley

Remembering the First Marina
in Navajoland

by

Wanda Morlan Eilts

Vishnu Temple Press
P O Box 30821
Flagstaff AZ 86003-0821
(928) 556 0742
www.vishnutemplepress.com

Dedication

The traditional Navajo pays homage to someone or to an event by remembering them in a story. Stories are told instead of writing a record of such memories. After many years of telling the story, I wanted to write it as my way of honoring and remembering the original employees of San Juan Marina and the Oljato community.

This book represents a historical memorial to them and their achievements. It will always be a real privilege to say we knew them and took this journey with them.

Thank you to:

Terrance and Laverne, Marilyn and Stanley, Harrison and JoAnn, Sam and Betty, Harry and Marilyn, Joe, Bud, Dennis and Carolyn, Rosie, Ben, Genny, Irene, Rose, Tully, Edgar and Rose, Richard, Dave, Ruth, Sylvian, and Jim and Jean Fatt.

May you always walk in beauty

Table Of Contents

Acknowledgements
and special thanks to:

Leona Goulding, who asked us to keep a diary and write about out lives in Monument Valley.

Jerry and Tena Sampson, who trained us in the marina business, had faith in our abilities and continue to support us through the good times and the bad.

Denise Morlan Graham, who has been a loyal sister and friend. Her brainstorming helped us get the title.

Peggy Manygoats, who teaches the Navajo language. She edited the Navajo words and provided proper translation and spelling for them. If they are still wrong, it's not her fault.

The National Park Service, especially Irv and Pauline, who thought the marina was a wonderful attempt to do the right thing for the Navajo people and supported the endeavor and us.

The Navajo Nation and Dave Johnson and Morrie Stewart who hired us and gave us the chance to manage San Juan Marina.

Friends and family far and near, who either visited the marina or supported our efforts and the writing of this book by rallying behind us and cheering us on.

Bette Killion, who made me believe that it was really possible to write a book.

Hazel Clark and Tom Martin of Vishnu Temple Press, who saw the potential of our book and had the patience to wait for us to get our story finished. Your encouragement was always positive when we thought we would give up.

To our God, who blessed us with this journey, the good health to see it through and the chance to write about it and share it with others.

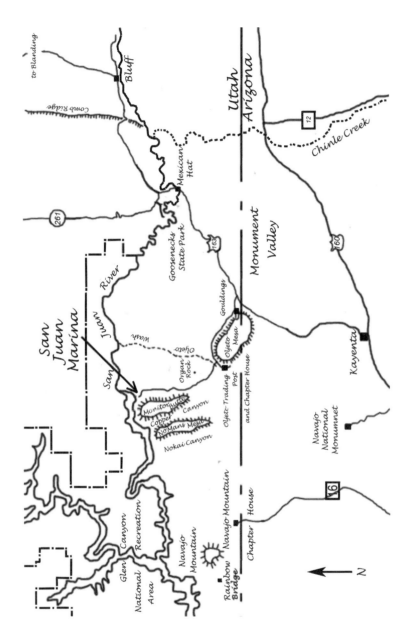

x

CHAPTER ONE
Spring 1987
The Beginning

MAY 31, 1987

We had seventeen more miles to go until we arrived at our destination. We pulled a six by twelve-foot U-Haul trailer behind our 1980 Ford car, a four-door, tan sedan. The isolated desert road was dusty, rough and had many curves. We slowed the car to a snail's pace because driving had become more difficult as gravel turned into the dirt of a seemingly scarcely driven trail. It was late in the afternoon and dusk was approaching. The western sky had turned into soft hues of purple and pink as the sun set behind us. Deep blue-gray clouds framed the distant mesas that rose in front of us. We were starting an adventure where we would be living with people who were different from us in age, in culture and in color. Turning to Terry, my husband, I asked if we were really doing the right thing. He winked and nodded with assurance, "Honey, where is that passionate pioneering spirit of yours?" he teased. Seeing his warm smile and his brown eyes twinkle, I knew that everything was probably going to be just fine.

The National Park Service (NPS) and the Navajo Nation had been working for years to design and complete a concession contract for a Navajo-owned and operated marina. It was to be built within the boundaries of the Glen Canyon National Recreation Area, which encompasses Lake Powell in southern Utah. In 1987 that plan was realized with the building of a marina on the San Juan River arm that joins the waters of Lake Powell at Paiute Farms. The marina would be located only twenty-six miles from the famous Monument Valley along the Arizona/Utah border. The new venture would be named San Juan Marina. The Navajo Nation had selected a local company, Utah Navajo Industries (UNI), to be the sub-concessionaire to manage the new marina. They, in turn, had hired Terry and me to be the property managers. We arrived at the marina after the construction phase had been completed. Having lived in this part of the west for many years, we were familiar with the general area. Driving past the ancient towering monuments and rock formations, we felt right at home. We would be living near Lake Powell, our most favorite place in the entire world. It was truly a dream come true. Life with Terry had turned out to be one exciting adventure after another. But little did we know that our decision to go to San Juan Marina (SJM) would be our best adventure yet.

One may ask why Terry and I would be qualified to participate in such a project. Terry's background as an electrician and plumber and my nursing qualifications gave us qualities that would be appreciated in any project we undertook. But it was our ten years' experience in the marina/resort business that made us good choices for SJM. Terry had worked his way through the ranks and had held many different jobs at several of the marinas on Lake Powell during those years. He had participated in all phases of houseboat rental and maintenance and had learned all phases of marina operation and management. He had also been a fishing guide, held a fifty-ton boat captain's license and was a service-orientated manager. I had advanced from a sales clerk to the position of purchasing agent for all marina operations. Our abilities to manage our employees in productive and amiable ways were admired and noted by our employers. We had earned praiseworthy and reliable reputations among the marina community and the NPS. Since the NPS controlled all of the marina operations and was in charge of the concession contracts on Lake Powell, it was truly an honor to be recommended by them for the positions at SJM. Also, we had worked with and made friends with many of the Navajo on Lake Powell. We enjoyed their quiet spirit and quick humor. It was very exciting to be invited to help them achieve their goals for their economic development. We had been chosen to teach them how to operate a marina and we were ready to begin the task.

Terry and I had come to the marina location a couple of weeks earlier to attend a job interview for the positions of managers. We were offered and accepted the positions that same day. We had met with men from UNI, Dave Johnson (President of UNI) and Morrie Stewart (Construction Superintendent) whom we had known from earlier marina days and felt very comfortable in working with these two men. However, during the two-week interval prior to our arrival, there had been a secret meeting of the board of directors of UNI. Dave and Morrie had been dismissed and Mr. K would now be our boss. UNI's five-member board of directors was made up entirely of Navajo men. Only the chairman of the board and the president were Anglo men. Mr. K (an Anglo) held the position of both president and CEO. It made us wonder what was going on with this company and whether this was something that should concern us.

JUNE 1 – 8

As mentioned, the construction phase of the marina had been completed when we arrived. The marina compound was a large area surrounded on the north, east and south by water. To the far right side of the marina compound, a wooden building, approximately forty feet wide and sixty feet long, sat on a hill above the water's edge. A covered porch at one end had several picnic tables setting under it. Inside, rows of shiny new shelves and a large empty walk-in cooler/freezer awaited our attention. They needed to be stocked with provisions such as groceries, tackle, ice, camping supplies, firewood and souvenirs for our customers. This building also held the boat rental office, an administration office and two restrooms. Operating policies and procedures needed to be created and written. Job descriptions needed to be assigned. Work schedules needed to be posted. There was clearly a lot to do.

Three hundred feet of new wooden docks sat in the water just over the hill to the right of the marina store. The docks had been anchored into opposing sides of the bay in which they sat with one thousand pound anchors. Two gasoline pumps were located on one end of the docks and a ten-by-ten-foot aluminum shed sat on the opposite end. The shed would house cleaning and replacement boat supplies, dock ropes, life jackets and the boat mechanics' tools and supplies. Four large cylinder tanks were located about twenty feet to the right of the store near the water's edge. One was for propane, one for water storage, and two ten-thousand-gallon tanks were for gas storage. A small four-by-four-foot wooden shed sat near the water tank and held the equipment needed to purify lake water into drinking water. To the left of the store, about fifty feet away, lay the launch ramp. About a quarter of a mile to the left of the launch ramp sat two large diesel generators enclosed inside a high fence. They were the only power source at the marina. Past the generators, about five hundred feet away and atop a small hill, sat our housing compound. Ten new seventy-foot mobile homes were arranged in a circle, with one end toward the center, not quite resembling the way covered wagons were circled in the old western movies. They were beige with brown trim and each had two bedrooms. One of the mobiles had been converted into a laundromat. A large bright blue storage tank (approximately eight-by-fifteen-feet), sat past the housing area. It held the raw sewage. To the west and a little behind our mobile home area was a fenced-in, dry storage lot. A large mesa, Monitor Butte, protected the marina from the west. It was an inviting and impressive site. There were no trees but it looked like an oasis in the desert.

Twenty-two Navajo men and women had been hired to fill the many positions needed to keep the marina running. Their ages ranged from eighteen to thirty and most of them were married with children. Ten of those employees lived as we did in the housing compound. The rest lived in and around the Monument Valley area, which included the little community of Oljato. This part of the Navajo reservation was noted for being very traditional in its customs and the way its people lived. Most of our employees had left the reservation after high school and had earned their degrees from various colleges across the country. They had come back to their homeland to live their lives in harmony with their Navajo customs. Job opportunities were scarce on the reservation, but it was more comfortable to return home and be without a job than live in the alien culture of mainstream America. Returning to raise their children in traditional Navajo customs and language took precedence over having money or positions in the Anglo world. Clearly, these people were glad to be employed at the marina. Money was desperately needed and SJM could provide not only a monthly income for our employees but also an economic future for the surrounding Oljato community. We were certainly pleased to be part of such a worthwhile endeavor.

The first week, Terry spent his time getting the marina organized, and I unpacked the U-Haul and got our house organized. One by one we met our employees and their families and tried to remember each other's names. We were curious and eager to learn all we could about each other. Daily, several black-haired, brown-eyed, reddish-brown round faces with broad smiles showing straight white teeth would appear at my door. The Navajo Welcome Wagon consisted of our female employees who brought along their children for us to meet. How precious the children were and even though they shyly hid behind their mother's legs, they would quickly accept the cookies or candy that I offered them. The ladies also brought us gifts of hand woven baskets, home spun rugs, and lovely turquoise jewelry. Often included with their visits were samples of their favorite Navajo foods, such as mutton stew and fry bread.

Mutton stew is a mouth-watering meat and vegetable soup made with chunks of mutton, squash, potatoes, carrots, cabbage and hominy. Fry bread is soft puffed-up bread shaped like a round tortilla that has been fried in lard in a skillet. It is eaten with the mutton stew with salt sprinkled on top or eaten alone with powered sugar or honey on top. It can also be eaten with chili beans, shredded cheese, chopped lettuce, sour cream, red salsa and green chilies on top; then it is called a Navajo Taco. Fry bread is our favorite Navajo food. It is simply delicious and it really does melt in your mouth. If your mouth is watering, see the recipe at the end of the book.

One day, two of our employees, Megan and her sister-in-law, Clara, spent the day trying to show me how to make fry bread. Megan, who worked as one of our cashiers, was a short lady just under five feet tall. Her wavy black hair was chin length and accented the smile that was always on her face. She was very talkative and she giggled all of the time. Clara, who was one of our houseboat maids, was very quiet and only spoke when spoken to. She was as tall as she was round and she too always wore a sweet smile. The girls, of course, had made fry bread since they were toddlers. So the shaping of the dough came easily to them. They took a portion of dough (about the size of a tennis ball), patted it, back and forth, turning it round and round, all the while stretching it to the size of a small plate. So I tried to do just as they did. But it was not as easy as it looked. I struggled with the dough, getting it stuck to my hands and fingers. Starting again, with more flour on my hands, I tried to go faster and the dough flew out of my hands onto the floor. Both girls giggled and giggled as I tried once more to pat out the dough. This time I stretched it too far and too thin and put holes into it. This was not a pizza I was making. It would take a lot of practice, the girls told me, if I was ever to make the proper size fry bread. But when it came to the eating of the fry bread, no one had to tell me how to do that.

JUNE 9 – 15

This week was very busy. We spent most of our time contacting vendors, setting up accounts for supplies and ordering goods for resale in the marina store. Since we had no regular telephone at the marina we had to drive to the nearest place that had one. This was the area known as Goulding's Trading Post near the community of Monument Valley. The only way out of the marina was on the same road we had come in on. It was actually a trail cut through red sandstone and it ran over rocks and large boulders and wandered through deep arroyos. It wound and curved around large sagebrush, tall prickly cactus and six feet tall cedar trees. Because of the terrain, the twenty-nine mile trip took at least forty minutes to navigate.

Since it was my job to deal with the purchasing and delivery of goods for SJM, I drove to Goulding's each day to place orders, pick up supplies and collect the mail. The road seemed long and uninviting. There were many washboard areas and loose rocks and gravel bounced off my dark maroon truck as I sped along. With the windows down, the warm summer wind blew through my hair, and I could feel the hot sun on my face. Fine, red sand drifted across the single lane road at several places and at one point a natural spring ran across it. Then there was the Oljato Wash to cross. This creek had no bridge to cross it. You just had to drive through it. Usually the creek bed was dry or ran with only a trickle of water. However, if it had been raining, there could be anywhere from one inch to eight feet of water running through it. One day, after a flash flood, I approached the water-filled wash and found that crossing it appeared impossible. I stopped my truck, got out and stood there pondering what to do next. How would I or could I get across? The water was muddy and ran very high and the creek had swollen to twice its width. There was a swift current and tree-sized debris moved rapidly past me. A friendly Navajo man pulled up in his truck and asked if I would like to cross the creek. I nodded and he motioned me to follow him. He said he remembered where the rocky high spots and the sandbars had been and knew we could get through. He instructed me to keep my foot on the gas pedal and not stop for anything. I got into my truck and started the engine. I put it in gear, pressed down on the gas pedal and went forward. My truck slid from one high spot to another and my heart pounded faster and faster. We finally reached the hard ground on the opposite side of the creek. We had safely maneuvered our trucks across without incident and waved at each other as we continued on toward Goulding's. Thus, a single trip to town could prove to be a dangerous undertaking.

The daily drive to Goulding's was lonely and a little scary at first. Here I was, a woman, traveling alone in an old battered truck, down an isolated road. However, as my trips increased and as time went by I began to absorb and appreciate the beauty of the desert countryside. Before long I welcomed the trip. Navajo children and women dressed in their brightly colored traditional clothing could be seen herding their flocks of white sheep and gray goats among the terracotta-colored hills. What a peaceful scene. I started to realize that to the Navajo, their daily chores were the fiber of their existence. Every day as I drove into town, I passed one of the local Navajo elders who would usually be riding his horse. We could easily see each other as he herded his sheep and goats near the road. We would wave to each other and although we never met, I felt that we knew each other well. *Hastıın* (Mr.) Tom looked so stately, straddling his roan horse and sitting on his red and black Navajo saddle blanket. He had no saddle. He was a very thin man and wore cowboy clothes, western styled multicolored shirts with long sleeves and dark blue jeans. Brown cowhide moccasins protected his feet. A crimson bandanna encircled his forehead holding back his long graying hair that was tied in a double bun at the back of his neck. His face was tanned and weathered and his wrinkled features always carried a look of pride and confidence. It was hard to guess his age but he must have been seventy or eighty. Even though his life probably was not as active as it had once been, it was apparent that he still enjoyed herding his beloved animals. He always reminded me of one of those old warriors in the western movies, the aging chief. This scene was so tranquil that every time I passed by I felt as if time had stopped. Years later we learned that our old friend had passed away and that his horse had been allowed to roam freely over the hills until it too passed away. Now they are together again.

JUNE 16 – 21

While at Goulding's Trading Post, I saw the local Navajo trading their wool, sheep, handmade rugs, handcrafted silver jewelry and borrowing money on their Old Pawn jewelry. Old Pawn is jewelry that has been held as pawn and is traded many times by its owner for goods or money. If the loan on the jewelry is not paid back, the jewelry is forfeited to the lender and can be sold. It is then called Dead Pawn. Many tourists look for Dead Pawn to buy as it is usually sold for a bargain price. At the trading post's only water spigot, men lined up to fill the large barrels in the back of their trucks. The local laundromat was crowded with women who gossiped as they watched their children play nearby. This was the place to socialize, do weekly shopping and get their mail. It was fun to be among them.

"Hello, I am Wanda from the new San Juan Marina.

Glad to meet you!" I had always been a friendly person, so I went about shaking hands with everyone I met at Goulding's. My firm and vigorous handshake got some very interesting smiles and giggles among my new acquaintances. It was politely pointed out that this was not the proper way to greet the Navajo. First, they do not make eye contact with each other. This is very impolite. Second, they do not speak any greeting until after the handshake has been completed. The Navajo handshake goes like this: a hand is extended slowly and the grasp is very light. It does not include the back part of the palm. The hand is then gently squeezed. One slow gentle down stroke and a slow release completes the handshake. The word, *yá'át'ééh*, meaning hello in Navajo is then softly spoken. The local Navajo were probably scared as I would grab their hands firmly and shake their whole arm up and down very fast like a pump handle! It is said that a Navajo will not refuse any outstretched hand, even that of an enemy, however, he may not speak any greeting to that enemy. After meeting and mingling with the people of my new community I felt their expressions of warmth and acceptance in their eyes. They welcomed me with their smiles. I was no longer skeptical of why we had come to this area.

It was 1987 and yet looking at how the Navajo lived, it seemed like one hundred years earlier. Many of the local people lived in earthen hogans. The traditional Navajo hogan is a circular or six-sided dwelling constructed of logs and covered completely with hard-packed dirt. The dome-shaped roof is formed of cribbed logs and is also covered with dirt. Originally the hogan lacked windows and was ventilated by a smoke hole in the roof and a doorway which always faces the east. The floor is made of hard-packed dirt and is covered by rugs. Most of our employees and their families lived in wooden homes or mobile homes on this part of the reservation. But many families also constructed a hogan near their more conventional dwellings for use in ceremonies, special events, family gatherings, or for their parents and in-laws to live in. Most dwellings, whether a hogan or not, did not have electricity, water or heat. Water and firewood were hauled to their homes from far away places by using their pick-up trucks.

The older women dress in the traditional Navajo way. They wear long, three tiered broomstick skirts and long-sleeved blouses both made of cotton or velvet. Their clothes are not fastened with buttons but with round turquoise brooches. As is still the custom, the woman is the head of the family and her wealth is determined by how much turquoise jewelry she owns and how many goats or sheep she possesses. Most of the older men wear blue jeans with cuffs rolled up and long-sleeved cowboy shirts, western styled boots and a black ten-gallon hat. Most of the older men and women wear their long black hair drawn into a double bun secured at the base of the neck. A piece of white yarn is wound around the middle of the bun to keep it secure. Even today this hairstyle is worn to remind the Navajo and their descendants of the struggles they endured in the 1800's. During that time Kit Carson had tried to round up all the Navajo in this area and march them to Fort Sumner in New Mexico for military confinement. However, many of the Navajo hid in the canyons near where SJM was now located and were not captured. By wearing this hairstyle, every member of the Navajo Nation and their descendants are reminded of their escape from capture and their fight for freedom.

Today the children and young adults wear short hair, Nike tennis shoes, and many of the same fashions as children who lived off the Reservation. But they also know and practice the traditional fashions, language and customs taught to them by their parents. Respect of family and family values are the roots of these Navajo with whom we had cast our lot.

We found the Navajo culture fascinating. While the rest of America approached the high tech twenty-first century head on, always hurrying physically and mentally, here in the middle of our vast nation was a complete culture different from the rest of the United States. The Navajo remained true to themselves and chose to be a society that practices what they have been taught through the ages. They not only have their own language, they also have their own government with its own president (chairman) and its own law enforcement agency, the Navajo Tribal Police. While managing SJM we had to comply with regulations of not only the Navajo government but also the local, county and state government, the Federal government and the National Park Service. It was quite a challenge trying to please everyone.

JUNE 22 – 23

Not long after we arrived at SJM, the employees asked us if a Blessing Ceremony or *hatáál* (a sing/ceremony in Navajo) could be held for their new marina. This ceremony was needed, they said, to give harmony, cleansing, and protection to the marina and its employees and to assure financial success. A *Hataałi* (a medicine man or singer or chanter) could be hired and the ceremony could take place right away. So, a local *Hataałi* was found and the Blessing Ceremony began. Dressed in traditional Navajo clothes, he spread a colorful, hand woven ceremonial blanket of red and black in the middle of the store floor. He began to chant in low tones. Each employee took his or her turn participating in the ceremony. Terry and I were asked to participate in this ceremony, although, often Anglos are not permitted or invited to do so. We were delighted and humbled and a little nervous. We did exactly as we were told. We did not want to upset the spirits.

Now a strange and unusual thing happened during that ceremony. While it was in progress, right in the middle of the store floor, in broad daylight, during normal business hours, many of our customers came and went. They shopped, went in and out of the store and walked around close to where the ceremony was taking place. Not one customer appeared to even notice what was going on. They showed no signs of stopping, staring, talking, and taking pictures or gave any other visible signs of recognition that they even saw us. Had we become invisible? This was the first of many strange and unexplainable events that Terry and I witnessed while living at San Juan Marina. We are not saying we believed in everything we saw and heard, but we are not saying we didn't. The supernatural was always a fascinating subject to us, and we were always open-minded to the possibility of new ideas. We did believe, however, that the *Diné* (the People) were indeed a very mystical and psychic people. You can decide for yourself.

JUNE 24 – 28

The fast and muddy San Juan River joined Lake Powell at the mouth of the bay that surrounded our marina. The more daring and hardy of our customers would raft down the rapids on the San Juan River and take their rafts out at our launch ramp. At this time of year, the rapids ran high and were very swift until the river met the quiet part of the lake, about a mile upstream from us. After that, the rafters needed a small motor to maneuver their rafts to the launch ramp. Without a motor it would take hours to paddle a few short miles.

It was 10 p.m. and Terry and I had just retired to bed. Dale, one of our security guards was on duty. Dale was usually very talkative and used his hands to emphasize his conversation. He always wore a broad smile that showed his amazingly straight white teeth. He was articulate in his speech and he looked very stylish in his round-rimmed glasses that sat below his black bangs. Dale was a very conscientious and capable employee, and that was why he had been chosen as a security guard.

A loud knocking at our door made us wonder what was up. Opening the door, Terry found Dale waiting. "Someone must be in trouble. There are lights flashing out there on the river," he said, pointing toward the marina. We knew this must be a true emergency for no one traveled the river at night. The darkness and the rocks in the water made it far too dangerous. Dale took a small boat out to the flashing light. By a two-way radio he relayed to us that help was indeed needed. After getting in contact with the local police by our limited telephone system, we contacted the Monument Valley Hospital, which was located only twenty miles away. An ambulance was immediately dispatched to the marina. After half an hour had passed, Dale pulled in a raft that carried an injured man and his three companions. Apparently, he had sustained a neck injury earlier that same day after diving into a shallow part of the river. His friends had administered some first-aid and had used duct tape to wrap his head and body to one of the seats in the raft. Their little motor had broken down upstream, and they had been paddling for hours trying to get help. They were so relieved we had seen their flashlight signals. Later, because of the nature of the injury, a helicopter was also sent from Kayenta, about forty miles away, to transport the patient. The man was flown about two hundred miles to the Flagstaff Hospital Trauma Center. We later received a letter from him saying that he had undergone surgery and that he had fully recovered and had full use of his body. He expressed his appreciation and gratitude for our help and kindness. That was a good day!

Our telephone system at SJM was quite a story in itself. Because of our remote location, we could not use regular telephones. The cell phone industry was still on the drawing board. We had a land-based marine radio that had the added capability of being used as a telephone. However, one had to be patient when using it and be sure to repeat the word "over" when you were through speaking. That way the other party knew that it was their turn to speak. The radio signals could only travel a one-hundred-mile radius and were constantly affected by the weather conditions. When the temperatures were high, the rising heat from the desert floor caused interference. If it was windy, there was interference. If it was raining or snowing, there was interference. In addition, not many people lived where the signals would be monitored or received. Virtually no one listened to their radios at night. There was only one person we could usually count on to hear us. Wesley, who lived in Blanding, Utah (which was ninety miles from SJM), ran the small local airport. As time went by, he fondly became known to us as our Guardian Angel. He would always hear our radio calls and convey our needs by regular telephone to those who could help us. This was just one more inconvenience we encountered and overcame while living at San Juan Marina, ... " over."

JUNE 29

The Navajo tribal chairman wanted to use two of our new fifty-foot houseboats for a weekend trip on Lake Powell. We guessed he wanted to impress his family and friends by showing off his newest economic development project. However, he chose not to pick up the boats at SJM but at Wahweap Marina, which was located down lake about ninety miles. A crew of six would be required to take and return the boats, clean them, cook the meals and attend to the needs of the chairman and his guests. Carl and his wife, Lucy, took one of the boats, and Fred and Ed took the second boat. Sandy and her sister, Jill, completed the crew.

Carl was our General Manager-in-Training at SJM. He was taller and thinner than most of the rest of our men employees. He was an intent listener and had a memorable way in which he looked into your eyes when you talked. He sort of squinted and looked through his glasses as though he was absorbing everything you said. His ability to communicate our instructions from English into Navajo was his best asset. Carl was not a talkative guy but understood what it took to get his fellow employees to understand and complete their tasks in an effective way. He always had a professional appearance and manner, and that made him an excellent candidate to represent SJM to the Navajo chairman. Lucy was one of the store cashier/clerks at SJM. She was an excellent cook and would prepare the meals on one of the houseboats. She wore her hair in a French braid or sometimes a ponytail high on the back of her head. She too wore glasses and had a very sweet smile and demonstrated the quiet, obedient and gentle spirit of a traditional Navajo wife. She would keep quiet and listen carefully. Carl and Lucy had two young toddlers, ages four and two. It was not practical for the children to go on this trip, but Lucy had no immediate family nearby to help take care of the kids, so I volunteered. I was delighted when she accepted my offer. We were glad to be acknowledged as family and trusted friends by our new employees. Even though we had a language barrier, the children were easy to care for and were perfect little guests.

Fred was one of our boat mechanics. This made him a good choice to send on the trip. He had a rugged look about him as his face carried many scars from childhood scrimmages. And, as many mechanics do, he always wore an old baseball cap and had grease under his fingernails. But he was a gentle man and always smiled and laughed quickly. He drove one of the houseboats and could fix any mechanical problem that might arise.

Ed, a quiet person who frequently stood with his arms folded across his chest, drove the second houseboat. He always looked like the "cat who swallowed the canary" as one eyebrow would arch as he looked at you. He was one of the dockhands at San Juan Marina and was an all-round fix-it man. Both he and Fred could maneuver and anchor the houseboats with safety and ease.

Sandy went on the trip to help with the cooking. She

was the Boat Rental Reservations Clerk at SJM. She was a short, shapely gal with a pretty, sexy smile that was accented when she tossed her shoulder length, curly black hair back from her face when she spoke. Sandy was articulate and confident in the way she expressed herself and communicated easily with our houseboat customers. She would be able to answer any questions that the chairman might have about houseboat rentals.

Jill, Supervisor of Boat Housekeeping, completed the crew and would help where needed as well as oversee the cleaning of the boats when the trip was completed. She too was a tiny woman (under five feet tall) who looked more like a little girl than a mother and wife. She was very thin and looked quite frail. But she was as sturdy as they come and was the hardest working person we had at SJM. When she and her maids finished cleaning the boats, you could literally eat off the floors. The crew would remain in Wahweap for a few extra days after the chairman's visit to clean the houseboats. Upon returning to SJM they reported that the chairman and his guests were impressed with our houseboats. He assured us that he would do everything he could to help SJM be a success for his people.

This adventure was significant in the fact that the Navajo have a belief that prevents them from sleeping on the water. They believe that they can only have harmony in their lives if they respect the natural resources of their environment. Not to show respect of the water could cause a water monster to bewitch them. Thus, if the crew slept on the water, they were not showing the respect they should, and they would become ill and require a 'sing' or healing ceremony to cure their illness. Our crew would be required to spend two nights and two days on the water during the trip to Wahweap. We didn't tell the crew how to handle the trip, but found out upon their return that each night they had anchored the boats to shore and slept on the land in sleeping bags. We always honored the Navajo beliefs and never questioned the way they performed their jobs as long as they got the job done.

Apparently, the chairman stayed on the houseboat during the day and slept in a local hotel at night. He and his guests didn't even take the houseboats out of the harbor and just sat on them at the marina docks. Well, to each his own.

JUNE 30

"Help! Help! There's a wreck. We need help!" It was 4 p.m. and one of our employees came running into the marina store. "A pickup truck has slipped off one of the curves on the road and several people are injured." Being a nurse, I went out where the wreck had occurred to see if I could help in any way. The driver of the truck had apparently been driving too fast and had lost control in the loose gravel on one of the sharp curves. The truck had rolled over several times and had thrown its occupants out onto the desert. It appeared that the three teenage girls and two teenage boys who had been in the back of the pickup truck were not seriously injured although I did administer some first-aid with a few Band-Aids. They were mostly just shaken up and dazed. The driver was also in a confused state, but he appeared to be ok. After a half an hour or so, when everyone was calm and collected, they all piled back into the pickup and went on their way. The next day it was all over our end of the reservation what a heroine I was. The Navajo grapevine was faster than any telephone. It was then I learned that the employees had given me the nickname of *asdzáán nımazí* (large, round woman.) I was indeed a large woman and was not offended by the new name. In fact, it meant a lot to me.

Terry had a new Navajo name, too, it seemed. Since he is a short man (about five foot and five inches tall) and he was the boss, the employees were now calling him *Hastıın ntsaaz*: Little Big Man. Move over, Dustin Hoffman.

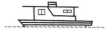

CHAPTER TWO
July 1987
Orange Tee Shirts

JULY 1 – 5

Have you ever had the privilege of meeting a living legend? Well, today we met Mrs. Harry Goulding. Leona (known as Mike by her friends) and her sheepherder husband, Harry, were the first white people to start a trading post in Monument Valley. In the early 1920's, they bought six hundred and fifty acres and set up a large white army tent. Amid primitive conditions, cold winters and hot summers, they started trading with the local people. Quickly they learned the customs and the language and they earned the respect of the Navajo people so their trading business flourished. Harry and Mike eventually left Monument Valley as their health began to deteriorate, but the trading post remains in their name and continues to be a major tourist attraction. Anyone who has ever traveled through Monument Valley or lived for very long around this part of the Southwest knows of this storied couple.

Mike Goulding came back to visit Monument Valley. A small, thin woman wearing a white summer dress sprigged with tiny, pink flowers approached our mobile home. Although in her late eighties, Mike had a steady and graceful stride. Her gray hair was cut short. A tan and weathered face held a smile and dark brown eyes twinkling from under her large-brimmed straw hat. When she spoke, the tone of her voice was soft but strong. After the formal introductions were made we sat down to get better acquainted. Terry and I quickly felt at ease in her presence. We listened avidly to the stories she shared about her life in this area. She related thrilling accounts about the people she had known and the many adventures she and Harry had encountered while living in Monument Valley. We enjoyed a light lunch of fruit, cheese and Navajo fry bread as the stories flowed. It was quite evident how much she and Harry had loved living here and how much she missed it.

After a long pause, Mike took my hand in hers and said, "I made this trip to San Juan Marina specifically to meet you and Terry. I have heard of what you are trying to achieve here and how much you love the people who live here. You and Terry are pioneers just like Harry and I were. You have an opportunity to help these wonderful people and become part of the history of this community. Destiny has brought you here."

My heart pounded in my chest as she spoke and I felt that indeed we shared a common passion. We continued to enjoy a visit that gave us a glimpse into the historically unique lives of Mike and Harry Goulding.

As Mike rose to leave, she stopped and looked straight into my eyes. "Would you do a very special favor for me, Wanda?"

I was instantly drawn into those comforting eyes and nodded my head up and down and said, "Yes, of course."

Tears began to form in her eyes and she told me she had always regretted never keeping a diary of her life and that she had never written about it. "Please keep a diary of your life here and write about it," she said as she tried to gain control of her emotions. "Somehow, I feel that Harry and I are sharing a common thread with you and Terry. By writing about the life you live here, I feel that all of our spirits will live on long after we are gone."

I suddenly felt very close to this sweet woman and gave her a long heartfelt hug. We never saw Mike again, but we continued to feel her spirit at SJM and among the people and the land she loved. That was when this book took its first breath.

When we lived in this area, the Goulding's compound included a full service hospital (sponsored and run by the Seventh Day Adventists Church), a KOA campground, a large fifty-room hotel, a grocery and supply store, a big laundromat and a post office.

Goulding's Trading Post continues to be a popular tourist attraction. It still stands upon the site where Mike and Harry first pitched that white army tent. The old wood and adobe building, which now holds a museum, was the Goulding's original home. That same building was used in many western movies. This was also one of John Wayne's favorite places and many of his movies were made here, such as *She Wore A Yellow Ribbon* and *Stagecoach*. Many of the fathers and grandfathers of our employees appeared in those early movies as well as in other movies that have been made there since. Monument Valley High School was and is still located near Goulding's and is still one of the most modern and progressive schools in the Southwest. There is also a small airstrip at the edge of Goulding's which is still used by the National Park Service and tourists alike to visit Goulding's and the Monument Valley area.

The smaller and lesser-known community of Oljato (`ooljéé'tó, meaning Place of Moonlight Springs) is situated about twelve miles northwest of Goulding's. In this small village a white block Chapter House is located near its center. A Chapter House is where local residents meet for town meetings and conduct government business. There is also another jewel in this remote area of Monument Valley. Oljato Trading Post, an 85-year-old rustic outpost, remains one of the last original institutions of its kind in the Navajo Nation. Its local traders still occasionally ride up on horseback and barter their goods. The old post has been on the National Register of Historic Places since 1980. If you are ever in the area don't leave without a visit to this special place.

JULY 6 – 12

Well, let's get back to our story. Our rental houseboats had been arriving steadily from California for weeks. Now, with our rental fleet complete, the real work began. Each of the houseboats had to be thoroughly cleaned. New motors needed to be put in and serviced. Handrails and other equipment, including anchors and ropes, needed to be attached to the boats. Also, all linens, cookware, dishes and other things had to be inventoried and stowed aboard. In addition, all of our powerboats, pontoon boats and fishing skiffs had to be cleaned and prepared for operation. All of our employees would be taking part in the boat preparation. There was, however, one small problem. You see, there is no word in Navajo for the word houseboat. Loosely translated *hooghan tsınaa'eetíoíí* means a box or log that floats on the water. So there were going to be some communication challenges. Not all of our employees could speak English. So the task of teaching our employees how to prepare the houseboats for rental fell to Jack, our Boat Rental/Dock Supervisor and his wife, Jill, mentioned earlier, who was our Houseboat Maid Supervisor. They had worked with Terry and me at other marinas and were our most marina-experienced employees. They knew what needed to be done and how to do it. So while we were trying to instruct, Jack and Jill were communicating our instructions in Navajo. By doing this, everyone could understand what needed to be accomplished in his or her own tongue. This took a lot of time and patience, and we learned that nothing was done before giving much discussion to each subject. After everyone had had time to ask questions, added his or her input, and had all this information translated back into English for Terry and me, then the task could be attempted. Terry and I learned that this process was just as important to the completion of a project as the project itself. Once a task was completed the first time, we did not have to explain it again or worry that it wouldn't be done properly. All jobs from then on were completed properly in record time. In one month we had outfitted and prepped seventeen houseboats, six powerboats, six fishing skiffs and four pontoon boats. Our entire fleet was ready for rent. Everyone looked forward to an exciting and profitable summer. How very proud we were of our employees. We told them so all the time. And Terry and I were learning valuable lessons of patience. Our time spent here was becoming very satisfying and worthwhile.

Terry and I had known Jack and Jill since their teenage years before they had married. We had worked with them at another marina on Lake Powell a few years earlier and enjoyed their company. Jack was of average height and build. He wore glasses over his brown eyes and round cheeks. What made Jack special was his very dry humor; he was very funny. He had a way of looking as sober as a judge all the while telling jokes that would make you split your sides laughing. It was Jack that first introduced me to Navajo humor many years before we came to SJM. I wanted to learn how to speak Navajo and asked Jack to teach me how to say "hello" in that tongue. He patiently worked with me to pronounce the word *hágoónee'* until I could use it proficiently. So I began to address all of my fellow Navajo employees with my new word. Immediately my greeting was greeted with giggles and confused expressions so I knew that Jack had not taught me how to say "hello." But what was I saying? I hurried to find Jack. Grabbing him by the nape of his neck, I said, "Hey, Bud, you have three seconds to tell me what *hágoónee'* really means."

He began laughing and said, "It means goodbye."

After that I always looked at Jack sideways, questioning whether he was telling me the absolute truth or not. Nevertheless, we became very close friends and Terry and I often referred to Jack as *shiyáázh* (son.) After he and Jill began their family, they also referred to us as *shinálí* (grandparents.) We were always included in their lives and they worked at other marinas with us after the days of SJM.

JULY 13 – 19

When we arrived at SJM, orange-colored tee shirts had already been chosen as the employee uniform shirts. It quickly became evident that the employees were not going to wear their shirts even though we repeatedly mentioned that it was the proper thing to do and that it was a rule that the NPS expected us to follow. (The NPS required uniforms to be worn by the marina staff so that they could be distinguished from the general public.) So when we asked the employees why they did not wear their uniform shirts, it was Bart, a General Manager-in-training, that spoke up. Bart had large broad shoulders and a square chest that he usually kept his arms folded across. His eyes had deep wrinkles that always went up at the corners in a smiling way. He always used the traditional Navajo way of pursing his lips when he spoke. He was a quiet man who gave a lot of thought to what he was going to say before he spoke. When he did speak, everyone listened as Bart's words usually held much wisdom and authority. He was respected among his peers. "The trustees [convicts] at the Tuba City Prison wear orange shirts and they are the ones who sweep the streets and do the crap jobs. Everyone sees us in orange shirts and they think we are prisoners and they tease us. We feel that this is a degrading way to dress," Bart related quietly and firmly.

Terry and I began to understand and didn't blame them. Explaining that we could not spend any more money on new shirts this year, we asked if they would consider a deal. If they would wear the shirts this season we would let them pick the color and types of shirts they wanted for the next season. Assured that they would not be thought of as convicts by our customers, all agreed to wear the shirts and from then on each employee wore his or her shirt every day. All of the employees had strong personal pride and wanted the marina to stand for everything that was good and proper. (P.S. Terry and I also disliked the color orange.)

JULY 20 – 31

If the reader has never been on a houseboat vacation, he may not know how the rental business works. The customer, or renter, pays a deposit to hold the boat and upon arrival the whole amount of the rental fee is due. Because there are so many things on a houseboat that can disappear or be stolen or broken by the renter, a physical inventory is done before the customer is allowed to take the boat out on vacation. Upon returning from his trip, the customer and a marina employee go through the inventory and the customer is then responsible for paying for any items broken or missing. If the houseboat is clean and there are no additional charges, the customer receives his deposit fee back. Of course, there were many excuses and stories that were given as to why something was broken or missing, but I think this next story was the best one we ever encountered.

A group of college boys had rented one of our houseboats for one week. Upon return, all of the front windows on the houseboat were gone. Not broken, just gone. Upon inspection, our employees could find not one bit of broken glass. When asked what happened to the windows, the boys told us that there had been no glass in the windows when they rented the boat. They started yelling at our houseboat representative who was trying to collect for the missing window glass and I had to step in to solve the matter. "Now, boys," I said, "you know there were windows in that boat. So just how do you explain their being gone now?"

One of the young men put his hands on his hips and spoke up, "Well, I guess it must have been one of those canyon ghosts that took them out during the night." He laughed and looked around at his mates like he dared anyone to challenge his statement. He continued, "When we woke up the next morning, the windows were gone. We are not going to pay for them and you can't make us."

I stepped up close to the counter that separated us and placed my arms on top of it. Looking squarely into his eyes I firmly informed him that he would indeed pay for the windows. "We can do this nicely or we can do it the hard way: but you are going to pay. You can be responsible and pay quietly or I can call the NPS Ranger who will be glad to help you pay. It is up to you."

As the boys griped and complained and swore under their breath and tried to devise a way to get out of paying, I felt the presence of two people, one on each side of me. Bart and Tommy had slowly and quietly come up from behind me and were standing by my sides with their arms across their chests. They looked straight into the boys' eyes and looked like they were ready for battle if need be. They were not going to let me be bullied. I raised my eyebrows and smiled as if to say, "Just what do you think now, punk?" Needless to say, the bill was paid without further incident. After the customers left, we all gave each other high fives and danced around giving war hoops. After all we were part of a clan and clan kin always stand together.

This is what I learned about the clans. Every Navajo belongs to a clan. They are groupings of the social structure of the tribe. The clan is not a kinship system connected by blood, but the system does use the terms of brother, sister, uncle, and aunt. Clans represent threads of linkage, which bind together Navajo who are not biologically related. A Navajo will always go out of his way to do a favor for a clan member. It is a solid, unwritten and unforgiving law. Also, the clan system helps contain proper marriage lines within the Navajo community. One may never marry within one's own clan or the clan of one's father. Such a marriage is thought of as incest. When it comes to marriage, the clan structure is strictly followed. So when Terry and I were given our own clan membership we knew we had been completely welcomed by our employees into their culture. We would be known as *Tábąąhá* or members of the Edgewater Clan (this being only an honorary title and a play on words because we lived by the water.)

Terry and I had been at SJM for about two months and were very satisfied with how well this project was progressing. It was amazing how quickly we had been received among our employees, and we felt as if we had inherited one big family. That is why we started to refer to our employees as "our kids." They were constantly coming in and going out of our house, at all hours, to say hello or talk or to eat food. We wanted them to feel welcomed but we found we had very little personal privacy. So we established a signal to let the kids know when they could visit. It was agreed that when the kitchen blinds were closed we preferred that company come another time. The kids thought this was just fine and, of course, they teased and giggled about just what we might be up to behind those closed blinds.

Our employees appeared quiet and reserved when we first met them, but we soon found they had a refreshing openness and positive outlook about life. They had an amusing and quick sense of humor, which was exhibited daily. They liked to play little tricks on us as well as on each other. For example, the kids wanted to help Terry quit smoking. So they hid an active smoke alarm in his desk. Every time Terry would light up, the alarm would go off and he would have to look to see where the buzzing alarm was coming from, thus not having time to finish his cigarette, much to their amusement.

Although each situation they approached was encountered with the same enthusiastic display of humor, thoughtful and thorough follow-up was given to each new assignment. Our employees never showed anger and the word "stress" did not appear to be in their vocabulary. How wonderful it was. (We Anglos could sure learn a lot from them. From birth to death, Navajo were not taught stress or saw examples of stress even though they lived in a land and environment that most Anglos would find totally stressful and unbearable.) When I would get stressed out about one thing or another at the marina, I did not want to lash out or say things to my Navajo kids. They might not understand my frustration or they might misinterpret my language if I got angry. So I would go down by the lake and throw rocks into the water with all the force I could muster until I got so tired from throwing rocks that my arms ached. By then, I would then be calm again. The kids would laugh at me and they must have known that I was venting my frustration but they never said a thing. It would have been impolite to do so. After a while, I didn't have to throw rocks anymore.

The universe, as viewed by the Navajo, is an orderly system of interrelated elements, an all-inclusive unity that contains both good and evil. With this concept of the universe, in which good and evil are maintained in interrelated harmony, maintaining that harmony or *hózhó* is the most important thing in the Navajo life. This is how he sees his success in life, not by how much money or status he has. In fact, it is a taboo to have too many material things as it may be viewed as being greedy. Harmony is the theme of the Navajo existence. This ceremonial prayer best sums up the Navajo philosophy of harmony:

> *When I go upon the road of life,*
> *There is beauty before me*
> *There is beauty behind me*
> *There is beauty around me*

There is beauty within me
That I, the son of the earth
The heavens
The waters
The sun
Have respect,
And the same have respect for me,
And those who come to me and talk with me
Have that same beauty.
All done in beauty.

CHAPTER THREE
August 1987
Washed Out Roads

AUGUST 1 – 6

The month started out very busy. All of our boats were being rented and customers were coming by the carloads to see the new Navajo Marina. They took pleasure in vacationing aboard the new houseboats. Time was savored as patrons spent hours exploring the San Juan River arm of Lake Powell. Revenues were climbing daily. Tee shirts, caps and souvenirs were selling like hot cakes. Shoppers quickly bought up the turquoise jewelry and hand-woven baskets and rugs that were made by local Navajo craftsmen. The employees worked hard at keeping the marina and the rental boats in top condition. The docks and houseboats were spotless.

We always had to be on our toes because we never knew who was watching or coming to visit SJM. First, there was the National Park Service itself whose staff kept a close eye on us. Since we were located on land set aside for use within Glen Canyon National Recreational Area, the NPS held the foremost authority over our comings and goings. We were regulated and governed by their NPS 48: a large, government-issued manual that outlined the operation and the policies and procedures one must follow when operating a marina overseen by the NPS. We referred to it as our "marina bible" and it had to be followed very, very strictly. Secondly, since the marina site was also considered part of the Navajo Reservation, it fell under the Navajo Nation's mandate. This included Navajo Nation Police for law enforcement. In addition, this part of the Navajo Reservation lay within the boundaries of the area known as the Utah Strip, necessitating compliance of Utah State laws. And not to be left out were San Juan County ordinances. Whew! Even in its conception, the marina project had enormous political relevance. We were being watched and visited by representatives from all of the above government agencies as well as senators, congressmen, members of the Bureau of Indian Affairs and delegates from the Department of the Interior. Because of our remote location, most of our official visitors would fly into and out of SJM aboard the Goose. It was a vintage seaplane, owned and operated by the NPS. Tug was the pilot. He was a well-seasoned flyer who wore an old WWII brown leather flight jacket. His blond hair could be seen peeking from under his matching leather cap. He had a movie star smile that went from ear to ear and made his passengers feel very comfortable. The old seaplane made the heavens rumble as it flew at a low altitude through the canyons. It made an impressive sight as it circled and then slowly descended like a large bird. Tug would land the plane on the lake with water spraying from under its wings. Then, slowly, the plane would waddle like an old gray-green goose up the launch ramp onto the red dirt of the desert and come to a stop only a few feet from the marina store. Its passengers would then jump out, "Ooohing and aaahing." Upon conclusion of their visit, the passengers would get back aboard the plane for departure. Tug would fire up the two engines and the Goose would slowly crawl back into the water. Starting at the far end of the bay, so as to have enough room for its climb, it sped along going faster and faster until eventually it lifted its large body up into the air, leaving water spraying everywhere. It must have been a thrilling ride.

One of the most important visitors at SJM was the NPS Concession Liaison. The contract between the NPS and the Navajo Nation required that monthly inspections of the marina be administered. Our jobs, the future of SJM, and future contracts between the NPS and the Navajo Nation hinged on the ratings received from these inspections. Pamela, a young, attractive Navajo woman, was our NPS Concession Liaison and Cultural Interpreter. One could always recognize Pamela even from a distance. Her shortness was disguised by the way she walked with authority, carrying her broad shoulders back and her head held high with confidence. She always pulled her beautiful black shiny hair away from her face, wearing it in a bun or letting it fall down her back to her hips. A lovely smile and high cheekbones made her eyes the first thing you noticed about her. They were large, chestnut brown, and looked at you with interest and sincerity. She listened closely, observed quietly, and ennunciated clearly. Having been employed by the NPS for many years, Pamela knew her job well. And she knew the NPS 48 from front to back and to the front again. She possessed the steadfast ability to fairly and prudently use her government training as well as her Navajo good sense and kind heart in making decisions when inspecting us. Her keen eyes never missed a transgression and she always checked that corrections had been made. Whenever a translator was needed, it was Pamela that accompanied us to the chapter meetings. She quickly became an important part of our family, not only as a NPS liaison, but she visited with us and got to know us during her off hours, too. Her love for us and our employees, and our love for her grew and grew. She believed in what SJM could do for her people. She celebrated and supported our successes as well as helped us face our struggles.

Her advice and interpretation of the NPS standards to the Navajo is still well known and favorably accepted today as it was during those days. Pamela is still very active in the affairs of her people and is still regarded as a highly influential woman. Her praises are sung all over the Navajo Reservation. She will always be a very special *sikis,* a friend.

AUGUST 7

It was a beautiful day, and the water was as smooth as glass when we noticed that one of the houseboats from Bullfrog Marina had entered our harbor. The boat was quickly tied to the gas dock, and soon there were several of the men hustling about fueling it. Terry could not understand why it took so many guys to put gas into this particular boat, so he wandered down the dock to see what was so important. As he approached the fueling station, he noticed that all the guys were attending to it like gas station attendants used to do in the 1950's for your car. They were washing the windows, cleaning the deck, and checking to see that the ropes were all in order. Terry noticed that one of the guys, Jack, was leaning against the boat and looking in the windows. Terry asked him what he was doing and all Jack could say was, "Uh, uh, I can't tell you, but all the guys have seen it too."

Terry asked what they had seen and was told that the boat was full of ladies and that none of them had any clothes on. It seemed that this boat was full of schoolteachers from Salt Lake City and that they were all nude and had been that way since they had left the marina where they rented the boat.

None of the ladies seemed to mind the guys looking and even came out of the boat when they left the dock and waved and said, "Thanks for the help," as they slowly motored away. It was going to be hard for the men to finish the jobs they had started that day while thinking of what they had just seen. There was rarely a dull moment at SJM.

AUGUST 8 – 14

Rain! Rain! Rain! Three solid days of torrential rains had descended upon SJM and the Oljato area. The desert sandstone and the gravel roads could not withstand the flooding that followed. After the rains stopped, Bart, Tommy and I traveled in a four-wheeled, forest-green, 1970 Jeep station wagon (which we affectionately named the Green Monster) out to see how much damage had occurred to the roads. Bart drove and Tommy sat on the passenger side. I sat in the back seat looking out the front window between their shoulders. Tommy reminded me of a little mouse in his actions. He was quiet and he kind of snuck around looking to see what he could find or scavenge. When he laughed his eyes would wrinkle up and his mouth would get sort of pointed and he would utter a little sound out of his mouth that sounded like a little squeak. One could almost imagine whiskers coming out from his wrinkled-up nose. Tommy was always a lot of fun to be around and he could add humor to any outing. We laughed and joked about this and that as we traveled down the road. However, as we came over the top of a hill and looked upon the storm damage in the valley below, we were not prepared for what we saw and the laugher stopped. Questions began to rise in my mind. Would our employees be able to get to work? How would we be able to get supplies to the marina? If our customers could not get into the marina either, then how much would our revenues diminish? If our business suffered, so would we.

Business had been increasing considerably and because many of our customers came in motor homes, many of them pulling large trailers with boats, it was imperative that we had good graded roads to the marina. We had been having trouble convincing the county road commissioners that the road to SJM needed daily grading and that many repairs were needed to improve it. On the way out to survey the damages from the storm, I took along my camera so I could play junior reporter and prove that the road did indeed need attention. Surely help would be forthcoming since I would now have pictures to prove my point. Maybe the pictures would even convince the commissioners that the road needed paving.

We stopped the Green Monster, got out and stood looking where our road ended. The desert had virtually reclaimed itself, and not one trace of anything vaguely resembling a road could be found. For at least ten to twelve miles ahead, all we could see were rocks and downed trees and bushes where a wide graded road had once been. What were we going to do? Even if there had been a faint trail to follow, the creek at the Oljato Wash would provide another obstacle. Instead of the small, easily crossed, lazy stream, an eight-foot wall of water would be crashing down the wash now. My stress level rose and I began to cry. "What will happen now? The marina will be ruined," I whimpered between sobs. Not really expecting an answer but maybe wanting some earth-shaking solution to suddenly comfort me, I turned to Bart and Tommy and gave them a hopeful look as if I expected them to provide the answers.

After a long silence that seemed like an eternity, Bart gently smiled and pursed his lips in Navajo fashion toward the wash. In his slow speaking manner he said, "Don't worry. The water will dry up in a couple of days and we will be able to cross over again."

In the pure wisdom of the Navajo, comprehending the solution was always simple. Let Mother Earth solve the problem in her own way and in her own time. Would my Anglo mind ever understand? Calmer now, I slowly smiled back at Bart, raising my eyebrows, knowing I had just learned a valuable lesson of how to handle life.

While we cleared away some of the smaller bushes and rocks so that the road could become somewhat passable, we reminded each other to watch out for rattlesnakes. They were often washed out of their dens by flooding waters. As quickly as this thought had been verbalized, the small clump of sagebrush that I was tugging on began to make the unmistakable "sssssssss" sound of a rattlesnake! I froze solid in my space. Looking down at the bush, I realized that only six inches existed between my outstretched hand and a coiled, medium sized rattler. Now I am a rather large woman and not very agile. But

I could have been a prize-winning pole-vaulter that day. Without thinking I jumped backward, about ten feet away from the snake, in one gigantic leap. Landing on my large rump with my legs sprawled out in front of me, I began screaming and swearing as I scooted myself backwards across the sand. Suddenly my scooting got my already sore rear stuck in a prickly pear cactus. Then I was on my feet, hollering louder than before and jumping up and down and round and round like I was dancing on hot coals. As I looked over at Bart and Tommy, I could see they were trying hard not to laugh. They failed dismally, and soon all of their efforts of constrained composure gave way to out-and-out thigh-slapping laughter. Indeed, they even fell to the desert floor and began rolling around, holding their bellies while laughing and giggling with glee. Was there no end to my humiliation? Well, indeed it must have been a funny sight to behold. I, too, began to laugh. Between spurts of laughter, Bart said that it looked as if I were going to jump right out of my pants! After that I was more careful while pulling bushes from the road. As we worked, we reviewed my snake encounter over and over and with each telling we laughed harder and harder. I never knew what happened to that snake. He probably slithered away to find a new home, thinking that these foolhardy, noisy humans were just too ridiculous.

As Bart predicted, the water went down, the county road crews brought out the road graders and before long everything at SJM was back to normal. It was a good lesson to learn: have faith and patience in Mother Earth.

After meeting with the San Juan County Road Department and showing the pictures I had taken of the rain-damaged road, I concluded that I had no future as a reporter. My ideas and suggestions were not welcomed with the enthusiasm I had hoped for. What was the hurry for a paved road out on the reservation, the commissioners had reasoned? Most of the paved roads around the Monument Valley area had taken twenty years to get that way. Why were we in such a hurry? No outsider was going to change the way things got done in San Juan County.

AUGUST 15

One thing we all had in common at SJM was a love of eating. We could always find an excuse to have a potluck or pitch-in dinner. When Terry and I had first arrived, food was used as a welcoming tool and a large Navajo taco party was held to celebrate our arrival. Whenever there was an excuse, any excuse, we had food. Now it was time to show our employees our personal appreciation for all the hard work they had done since the marina had opened. So, we scheduled a get-together one evening after working hours and invited all of our employees and their families to come to the marina for a cookout. We had found out quickly that in the Navajo culture it was customary that when one was invited to enjoy a meal, the entire extended family was invited too. You never knew just how many people might show up.

This would be the first opportunity Terry and I had to meet many of the parents and families of our employees. We wanted to make a good impression on them. So I spent hours preparing mounds of fresh potato salad, several large roasters of hickory smoke-flavored pinto beans and we bought enough thick T-bone steaks to fill the bed of a small pick-up truck. Needless to say, we were excited and a little nervous as to how we were going to communicate with our new friends as most of the parents of our employees did not speak or understand English. We would certainly rely on our employees for help with the interpretation.

One of our visitors included *Hastin* Jim Fatt. He was the father of our employee Bart. Mr. Fatt was a respected leader of the Oljato community. His ancestors, who were of Paiute descent, had lived in the canyons from Navajo Mountain in the east to the San Juan River in the west for centuries. They had farmed the sandy land along the San Juan River in this area, thus the name Paiute Farms. The marina actually sat upon land that had once been included in Jim's personal grazing rights. Jim's wife, Jean, had been born on this land and had lived all of her seventy-four years here as well. But the National Park Service annexed it when Glen Canyon National Recreation Area had been established. Of course, like others he had received no recompense for it. Jim was not bitter about the marina being on his land. On the contrary, he was always interested in all of the employees (many of his own relatives and clan relatives worked at SJM) as well as the progress of the marina. He was well liked and honored among the Oljato neighborhood. He led an active role in the community and chaired the chapter house meetings. When Jim Fatt spoke everyone listened. His word was the law. This was certainly one person we really wanted to impress and to gain his support for the marina cause. We wanted to get to know Mr. Fatt and be able to talk to him about the marina and to learn what it meant to him and his people, but we had been told that Jim could not speak English. It appeared that he needed an interpreter to be able to talk with us.

Back at the barbecue, Terry manned the grills and I bustled about making sure our employees and their families kept their plates full. As I passed Mr. Fatt, I asked him if he had gotten a steak. He looked at me, raised his eyebrows and shrugged his shoulders. I motioned to him by putting my hands to my mouth and then pointing to the grill, to go over to Terry and get a nice big juicy steak. Jim looked like he understood. I bustled around the food and our guests and again made my way back to Mr. Fatt. I noticed that there was still no steak on his plate. Again I asked him if he had gotten a steak. He shrugged his shoulders again, and I made signs for him to get a steak again. He smiled and I thought he understood. About ten minutes later, as I passed by Mr. Fatt, I saw no steak on his plate. What a bad hostess Mr. Fatt must think I am, I thought.

Bart was nearby, so I asked him to tell his dad to be sure to get a steak. So Bart interpreted my instructions to his dad, and I assumed a steak was gotten. Later, I noticed that Jim still had no steak on his plate and, when asked, he again shrugged his shoulders and smiled. This time I personally went and got Jim a steak. When it appeared that everyone was finishing up and it looked like the food was almost gone, I went over where Mr. Fatt was sitting and asked if his belly was full. I made rubbing motions in a circle over my stomach as I stuck it out in front, and puffed up my lips like a blowfish to show my being full. Jim shook his head back and forth.

"No? " I said. "Then come with me." I grabbed Jim by his arm and led him over to Terry and asked Terry to give Jim the biggest steak he had left. Jim smiled in thanks and went off to enjoy his food. It looked like the barbecue had been a success, and although we had not had the chance to sit and visit very much, everyone said, *"Ahéhee' dóó ayóo alkan,* Thank you. It was good," and took all the leftovers they could hold and left for their homes.

As Terry and I cleaned up and then sat down to reflect, we expressed our hope that we had been good hosts. I told Terry about how I just couldn't get Mr. Fatt to eat.

He looked at me sideways and laughed, "Are you kidding, Wanda. Jim had at least five steaks to eat tonight." When I told Terry the account of how I had tried to make sure Jim had a steak, we both doubled up in laughter. Jim is probably still chuckling at the success of his prank.

AUGUST 16 – 19

Now would be a good time to discuss the water and sewer systems. The reader may ask why this subject was so important to the marina. Throughout the chapters ahead, the answer will become quite clear.

The location of SJM at Paiute Farms was selected as

a temporary marina site until a permanent site could be chosen and acquired. Now, this fact was very important despite there being no potable water available at Paiute Farms. Also, because of environmental considerations and because it was a temporary site, the NPS would not allow a sewer lagoon to be installed on the property to dispose of sewage. So, two portable systems were brought in to meet our water and sewer needs. First, was the water treatment plant. It used chemicals and filters to turn muddy, sandy, bacteria-filled lake water into clear, clean and safe drinking water. This was how it was supposed to work. Water was pumped from the San Juan River through hoses into a filtration system. Then the water was circulated through several filters, as gauges monitored its clarity and purity. Next, the water passed through several different chemicals, such as chlorine and fluoride, to purify it further. A six-thousand-gallon tank, located near the marina store, would hold the potable drinking water. The water quality would be tested weekly and the results would be given to the required state, county and NPS agencies.

Secondly, another portable package plant dealt with the sewage. Raw sewage was sent to a large, two-compartment processing plant by three pumping stations called lift stations via pipes throughout the marina. The first storage compartment on the plant used blades powered by motors to mix the sewage and break up the solids and liquefy them as much as possible. Chemical enzymes were added in this section to assist in the breakdown. After that, the sewage was pumped into the second compartment, which mixed air with more chemicals, causing any remaining solids to sink to the bottom. The effluent liquid, which was good non-potable water, could then be pumped to a spray field for evaporation.

The concession contract with the NPS stipulated that both systems receive state and county approval before they could be used on a daily basis. Approval was to be obtained as soon as possible. Otherwise the NPS would be forced to close the marina for having unsafe health conditions for public use. But getting approval for these two systems was not simple. Weekly water samples were taken from the water tank and the NPS picked them up to be tested. The results came back showing that the water being used was indeed good water. However, the State of Utah said that since no water plant of our kind had ever been used and approved within the state, and since there was no record showing the longevity of its use, they could not approve the water system. In addition, the sewer plant could not be approved unless the water plant was approved. In conclusion, San Juan County was not going to approve anything unless the State of Utah did so first. Until the two systems were officially and satisfactorily approved, we could not use them. What were we to do? The answer? We would have to haul water into the marina and haul the sewage out.

John was our Sanitary Engineer-in-training. He was the largest of our employees with broad shoulders and a barrel chest. He looked as if he could have been a rough, tough center for a football team. But his quiet voice and his gentle, kind ways betrayed his teddy bear character. His laughter was always catching, and he loved to play jokes better than anyone. But it was John and his team (which included any employee who was not busy doing something else) that took charge and made it their job to meet our daily water and sewer needs. They had to haul water into the marina and haul sewage out every single day. The nearest water could be found at a water line located about fifteen miles from the marina. The sewage was taken and dumped into a man-hole near the Oljato sewer lagoon. So, how did we get the water into the marina, and how did we get the sewage out?

The marina owned one diesel truck and two tanker-trailers. Both tanker-trailers were silver and appeared to look exactly alike except the one that was used for water had a partial picture of a girl on its side. This trailer was always used for hauling water, and the other was always used for hauling sewage. However, we had a constant fear that perhaps the employees would accidentally get them confused. John would regularly tease us and tell us that, "Oops, there has been a mix up. We accidentally put the water into the sewer truck!" Of course this would instantly cause Terry and me to jump up and exhibit strong and explosive reactions. These were always met with smiles and laughter of a successful ruse having, once again, been played on us. Every day, it took two loads of water to fill our storage tank and two tankers of sewage to keep the sewage tank empty. This put a lot of wear and tear upon our diesel truck as it was constantly being driven back and forth on the rough road to Oljato. Four round trips of seventeen miles each way equal 140 miles per day. This was every day, seven days a week and fifty-two weeks a year. As our business steadily increased, so did our water and sewage hauling. The marina included ten mobile homes occupied by employees and their families, a small laundry used by employees for personal use, as well as the houseboat linen, a store with two much-used bathrooms, and seventeen houseboats (each of which had to be filled with 100 gallons of water and each held 100 gallons of sewage which had to be pumped out daily.) Our houseboat business had been doubling and even tripling. So the reader can easily see how important the water and sewer situation became and how it consumed much of our time.

AUGUST 20

SJM, like most marinas on Lake Powell, was located in an isolated area. Employees usually did not have the luxury of having the same days off every week or even having any days off for long periods of time. The marina manager never had official days off as he or she was on call twenty-four hours a day. Such was our life at SJM. We had worked from May until now without any time off for ourselves. But today was to be different. Terry and I were invited to join our co-workers from our reservations office in Blanding, Utah for a picnic and cookout. The Blue Mountains near Blanding would be the location of the get-together. Our hosts traveled ahead to prepare the campfire and eating arrangements. When we arrived, long wooden picnic tables were dressed in red-checkered tablecloths and set in a long row among the tall pines. In the nearby meadow, firewood had been gathered for later use and a net had been set up for volleyball. Barbecue grills were lined up near the picnic tables and we could see the smoke coming up from them and smell the mouth-watering aroma of steaks being charcoaled. Black cast iron kettles held homemade baked beans and crispy fried potatoes. We filled our plates with fresh crunchy salad which we ate while we waited on the steaks. A plague of locusts could not have done better justice. The children, and those adults still able to move after eating, played volleyball in the meadow. As dusk filled the purple skies overhead and the dark shades of evening approached, we could hear the call of the crickets and night birds. The air began to cool so a campfire was started. The now-familiar aroma of burning pinyon and juniper filled the air, and we sat close together on cedar logs enjoying the company of our new friends. A full moon rose in the sky over us. Occasionally a coyote was heard howling his unmistakable lonesome call. Someone brought hand-cut roasting sticks to the fire, and marshmallows were soon melting over the red embers. The conversation centered upon our common interests of SJM and getting to know each other. We wished our kids could have been here to share this wonderful evening. But they were watching over their marina, and we knew that it was an important part of their management preparation. After all, we were there only to train them and then we would be gone. Pride filled my thoughts but my heart suddenly felt a little sad. We knew the day would come when their training would be finished, and we would have to leave our kids. A strong connection to these

Navajo and their culture had already begun to form between us, and I was not looking forward to that day. But for now, there was still plenty to do, so we did not take time to worry about the future.

AUGUST 21 – 28

The daily trials of hauling water and sewage were not the only utility problems that arose at SJM. One day the electricity throughout the entire marine compound began to fail. Gradually we had no power to continue operating the marina. Terry immediately went to work trying to find out why. The generators were producing enough power, so that was not the problem. As it turned out, there were numerous breaks in the electrical wires that ran underground throughout the marina area. Terry discovered that not only had the wrong type of wiring cable been used, but that it had been buried only a few inches under the topsoil. It should have been enclosed in steel conduit and buried at least a foot or more into the ground. The sharp rocks in the soil were cutting the wires to shreds causing outages all over the compound. We supposed the managers in charge of the marina's construction thought it wouldn't matter since SJM was only a temporary site. Well, it did matter. The marina had only been open for four months. Since we were in such an isolated area, it was a task to find an electrician who would come right away to make the needed repairs. It looked as if we would be without any electricity for at least a week, and the cost to re-wire the entire marina would exceed $9,000! Why had it not been done correctly the first time? we wondered. Well, it was too late now and we had to keep the business going. After all, Terry and I were living among people who did not have electricity or air conditioning or any of the electrical gadgets and conveniences to which we were accustomed. If they could survive, so could we. Luckily I remembered my upbringing on a midwestern farm in the 1950's and knew how to make do.

Even today, as I write, most of the Navajo people in the Monument Valley/Oljato area burn wood in their stoves, use their trucks to haul water from far away places and live much as their ancestors did over a hundred years ago. There are plans to bring electricity to the area and a few folks do use solar batteries to provide electricity to be able to enjoy luxuries such as light bulbs and VCR's in their homes. Even though more and more Navajo housing projects are being built, many traditional Navajo still prefer to live in log and earthen hogans.

AUGUST 29

Do you remember the old saying, 'When it rains it pours?' Today's events made us feel that SJM was having a streak of never-ending troubles. It seemed that every time one problem was fixed another reared its head. Because we did not have any electricity at our laundromat, Terry and I had to take all of the houseboat laundry to be washed at the nearest one, which was located at Goulding's Trading Post. We were also going to pick up some supplies, make some phone calls, pick up the mail and do errands. Planning to be gone from the marina for most of the day we left very early. The skies, although cloudy, did not appear to be threatening, nor was it raining. A CB radio had been installed in our truck and we could now keep in constant contact with the marina employees when leaving the marina property. The afternoon sun was low in the western sky as we headed down the Paiute Farms road and back toward SJM. Suddenly we heard a loud, frightened, quivering voice on the CB radio calling out, "Help! Help! This is Sandy at SJM. Please help!" We listened as she excitedly explained that a tornado-like wind had suddenly come out of nowhere and had moved all of the houseboats and the gas docks out into the marina bay. Sandy said it appeared that they might take off and float down the river. Marina managers always fear strong winds because its effects usually included damage and danger. Sure enough, the anchor cables securing the docks had broken and the gas lines at the gas pumps were the only things holding the docks together. The docks were straining against the force of the river current pulling on them, and we feared that if the gas lines broke, we were in real peril. Terry calmly spoke to Sandy over the CB giving her instructions to relay to the rest of the employees. Sandy's voice began to calm and she quickly and efficiently passed on Terry's instructions. The employees on the docks followed every detail that Terry gave and by the time we arrived on the scene, everything was under control and no one had been hurt. However, there was a lot of damage to the docking system and we discovered that this was another temporary building project gone awry. The docks had not been built or anchored properly in the first place so it was no surprise that the winds had played havoc with them. We were able to get the repairs done quickly but the cost well exceeded $4,000. These major expenditures were taking big chunks out of the operating profits of the marina. Again, if only things had been installed correctly the first time, maybe these emergencies would not have happened. Well, it was not our fault. Remember, Terry and I were hired and started at SJM after the construction phase had been completed and had not been given the opportunity to contribute any input into how the construction should be done. What would happen next?

AUGUST 30 – 31

SJM had its own security people. Also, we had a NPS Ranger who lived on the property. In addition, several policemen from the Navajo police station in Kayenta patrolled the area at least twice a week. Because there was only one road into and out of SJM, we enjoyed a secure feeling that any major crime could not penetrate our little neighborhood. But every community, large or small, has its minor law offenders. They are people who are just aching to get into trouble with mischievous antics and troublesome pranks. Usually alcohol is involved and, after a strong reprimand, a small fine suffices as punishment.

Terry had gone to Albuquerque, New Mexico, for a meeting with our boss, Mr. K, and would be gone for a couple of days. The NPS Ranger was away from the marina on his day off and the Navajo police were not expected this evening. I alone would be responsible for the marina. Our scheduled security person, Sally, had made arrangements to arrive late this night. Sally was a small girl who wore her long black hair in a French braid. High checkbones framed her beautiful smile of white, straight teeth. Sally always said what she thought and usually stood with her shoulders squared back with her hands on her hips. She was a tomboy and an experienced horse rider. Her barrel racing had made her tough and she could handle any emergency. She would arrive about nine p.m. for work duty. All appeared quiet at the marina as I prepared for bed. About eleven p.m., I was suddenly awakened out of a deep sleep as Sally pounded loudly on my front door.

"Someone is shooting at the marina store and houseboats," she panted, trying to catch her breath. What on earth was this all about? Why would anyone want to shoot at our houseboats? It was clear to me that professional help was needed to get this situation under control before stray bullets damaged our property or one of us. Still clad in my long cotton nightgown, I crouched as I ran next door to Jack's trailer. He too was soundly sleeping and it was hard to wake him up. We in turn woke Carl. They were the only men on the property I could call on for assistance as everyone else had left for their days off. The only telephone available for us to call for help was located at the marina store. Under the cover of darkness, we all carefully walked to the marina store and as we approached it we actually heard bullets make whizzing sounds as they passed by our heads! We crouched and went into the store. We crawled on all fours, one behind the other, through the darkness until we found the telephone to call for help. We eventually contacted the authorities in Blanding and they in turn called the Navajo police. Now there was nothing to do but wait until help could arrive. How long would it be, we wondered as we sat huddled together on the cold concrete floor. Were we going to be killed sitting there in our underwear and nighties? It was times like this that I wished we did not live in such a remote area.

About forty-five minutes passed before we saw head-lights approaching the marina store. Navajo officers immediately summed up our predicament and took off into the darkness of the desert to resolve the situation. They were able to quickly find the shooters even though there were no lights or roads to follow through the rough and sandy terrain that existed around the marina area. Our intruders turned out to be a local schoolteacher and her student. They had consumed too much beer and were apparently showing each other a good time. They swore they were only using a shotgun to scare away coyotes. They emphatically insisted that they were not shooting at the marina or anyone there. The police officers escorted them to the local calaboose to sleep it off, and we all returned to our warm beds to slip back into a welcomed feeling of peaceful security. Well, there was always something exciting happening at SJM and Terry had missed the excitement this time.

CHAPTER FOUR
September 1987
Chapter Meetings

SEPTEMBER 1 – 7

"If you build it, they will come," is the quotation from a popular movie. This applied to SJM as well. People were coming by the dozens, from everywhere, to rent our houseboats and to visit the marina. Even though SJM had only been open for business for three months, revenues had exceeded all expectations. They had already gone beyond the $500,000 mark! Now Labor Day weekend was here. Since it is traditionally one of the busiest holiday weekends in the life of a marina, additional revenues would only make our already impressive totals look positively unbelievable. We were ready. The store was completely stocked with ample supplies of ice, tackle, souvenirs, groceries, camping goods and snacks. The rental fleet was in shipshape condition. The gasoline storage tanks were full and the fuel pumps on the docks had been repaired. The electrical and dock repairs were finished and even the sewer and water systems were behaving. The fishing was improving and the weather forecast indicated warm and sunny weather with no wind. Our employees knew their jobs and we were as ready as we could be. Both the NPS and the Navajo Nation (as well as our boss, Mr. K) were pleased with all of the progress at SJM thus far. All of our inspections had received excellent ratings and we were gaining the reputation on Lake Powell of giving quality and friendly service to our customers. Terry and I were truly glad we had come to SJM. We agreed that even though the problems, at times, had been many and the work hard, the satisfaction we now felt made it worthwhile. We were very proud of our employees and, most importantly, they were proud and confident of themselves.

As predicted, the weekend was a huge success. Over twenty-one thousand gallons of gasoline (all that was in the storage tanks) were sold. All of our boats were rented. The overstocked shelves in the store were now practically bare. There had been no law enforcement problems, the fishing was great and there had been no serious accidents. However, there had been one interesting houseboat incident that is worth mentioning.

"Houseboat 7 calling SJM, Houseboat 7 calling SJM," came the call over the marine band radio. Terry answered the call and asked what he could do for the person calling. "We seem to have had an accident and wanted to tell you about it," came a response.

Terry stood at the window just looking out and not saying a word. Then he asked what type of accident had occurred and if everyone was okay or if there were any injuries. "If there are injuries, we will call the NPS and have a ranger dispatched to your location to assist with the injured person," Terry informed them.

After a short pause, a voice came over the radio and said, "No injuries, but your boat is not that lucky." Terry asked what had happened and was told that the driver of the boat had been talking with his wife and kids and not paying attention to where he was going. As he talked he was slowly turning the steering wheel and had turned the houseboat directly into a solid rock wall.

Terry asked what type of damage was done and the man at the other end said, "Well, it seems that the cabin on the houseboat has been moved a little." Actually it turned out that the cabin had been moved over three inches back on the deck. And from that day on, Houseboat 7 never really seemed to track through the water correctly.

When the customer checked in with the boat, all he could say was, "I'm sure glad that this accident didn't occur on my job or someone would have been very seriously hurt or even killed."

Terry asked the man what type of work he did and was shocked when the man said, "Well, I'm a pilot for a major airline, and I sure hope that this is the only accident of this type that I ever have." This was not the only accident that occurred with our boats, but most were not serious.

The main objective of our being hired at SJM was to train twenty-two Navajo men and women in the skills of marina operation and management. The NPS and the Navajo Nation had projected that the employees would be able to take over the tasks of running the marina themselves within twelve to fifteen years. The progress that had been made in only three short months was outstanding. If they kept it up and with the experience they were gaining, they would be very capable managers. The employees were constantly asking lots of questions and we tried to answer them as honestly and thoroughly as we knew how. They had an inexhaustible energy when it came to learning. And they were eager to put into practice everything they had learned. We were seeing the fruits of our labor and it was exciting and reassuring. All of the time-consuming training that had been invested in our employees was paying off. The employees were now putting into practice all the new skills they had learned. These important skills also provided the wherewithal to obtain jobs in other places of employment if they ever left SJM. Four of the young men were being sent to outboard motor school to become certified outboard motor mechanics. Five of the young women had learned accounting procedures and were taking over not only cashier responsibilities but had learned how to work with vendors and could purchase goods for the store. Four of our young men were now considered competent in the operation of the water treatment plant and the sewer plant. Three other women employees achieved housekeeping expertise. Five of our men could make maintenance repairs of all kinds as well as do diesel generator maintenance. Two of our employees held the highly responsible job of security officers. And all employees were cross-training in different areas of marina operation. Finally, they were all learning management techniques that could be used throughout their working lives.

Years earlier during the learning and training period of our marina life, we met and worked for Jerry and Tena Sampson. These two wonderfully wise people had become our marina mentors and had taught us everything we had come to know in the marina management world. They had once told Terry and me, "Never be afraid to teach all that you know to others, so when the time comes, you can move on." Did they somehow foresee our coming to SJM?

SEPTEMBER 8 – 14

SJM had become a welcome addition to an already active Navajo community. The children of our employees were involved in many school-sponsored sports and activities. The parents and extended families of our employees held local community offices, and our employees willingly and dutifully supported and took part in the local government affairs. So it was not surprising when SJM was asked to participate in the Monument Valley High School homecoming parade. Most of our kids had graduated from MVHS. In addition, it was a good way to advertise and promote business at SJM.

When our kids put their heads together, the creative juices would overflow. A sixteen-foot aluminum fishing skiff was taken and decorated from bow to stern. It was completely covered with handmade tissue paper flowers of gold and blue (the school colors.) Silk ribbons of red, white and blue were attached among the flowers. A brightly painted arch, two foot wide, was made out of cardboard and attached to a strong supporting wire to resemble a rainbow. It stretched over the boat lengthwise. Under the rainbow, hung a yellow banner with bright blue lettering supporting the favorite school football team. *Go Cougars – Sail to Victory* was printed on both sides of the banner. Sandy's little twelve-year-old girl, named Leeta, had been chosen to be the homecoming princess. Her petite frame was clothed in a white traditional Navajo-styled dress and a small rhinestone tiara set on top of her waist length, black, shiny hair. Leeta presented a shy but beautiful smile as she waved to the crowds. Sandy was a very proud *shimá,* mother, that day. Several of our employees rode in the float that was pulled by a black pickup truck. They threw candy to the children that lined the parade route. Other employees walked along beside the float passing out SJM brochures. What an enjoyable and easy way to advertise. Everyone had a good time and our entry took third place. We gave the twenty-dollar prize money to little Leeta.

Another exciting event took place shortly after the Labor Day weekend. The much anticipated satellite dish finally arrived. One of the modern inventions that we all enjoyed was watching television. However, since we lived in such a remote part of the world, television transmissions could not be received on conventional equipment. Can you imagine such a thing in these days of high tech? Fall would be approaching in about a month and the daylight hours would be getting shorter. Our TVs would help span the hours from after work to bedtime. Now we could be included in the world outside of SJM, and we would feel less isolated. So, the day the satellite dish arrived, we happily took to our homes to try out our new toy. During the months ahead, especially in the evening hours, and since very few of our employees had any TV's at home, we always had a living room full of employees and their families who wanted to watch it. We would pop corn and laugh and cry at the various shows and movies we watched together. These times were some of the happiest hours spent at SJM with our kids.

SEPTEMBER 15 – 21

Rumors always seemed to linger longer than any truths. It was the same in the Monument Valley/Oljato community. Because there were many English words that did not translate into the Navajo language easily, the rumors may have lost a lot of their original content. This gave them a new dimension so their meanings got more confused and misunderstood. Something that may or may not have actually happened would be discussed among the Navajo community for months and months.

Our kids had been telling us that the people around the Oljato area were upset because of the many rumors they had been hearing. It was circulating around the community that our employees were allowed to drink alcohol on the job which was not true, of course. Other rumors apparently included the personal misconduct of our employees while on the job. Not true either. The Navajo people in the Oljato area were some of the most traditional on the reservation, and the thought of their children being exposed to alcohol was very upsetting to them. We did not sell alcohol of any kind at SJM because we were part of the Navajo Reservation, and it was illegal to sell or even to possess alcohol on the Rez. We even advised our customers of this law and encouraged them to not bring alcohol with them when they came to rent their houseboats.

To dispel some of these rumors about SJM, a chapter meeting was planned by the local elders. We were invited to attend. Terry was also asked to address the chapter members on the progress of SJM and we were told there would be a question and answer session. Communication of any kind was always good and Terry hoped to secure their support through his report.

The chapter meeting was scheduled for 10 a.m. However, it was midafternoon before enough people had drifted in to form a quorum. Remember we lived on Navajo time, not by the clock. The small white block building (the Chapter House) had no air conditioning, so all the doors and windows were open to allow the gentle warm breeze to flow through. Old wooden plank floors creaked as we walked into the main part of the building. The large room had no partitions, and there was a wooden stage area up front. There were chairs, old and new, of all descriptions lined in rows for seating. Even a few worn church pews made up the two front rows. The smell of fresh brewing coffee mixed with the aroma of burned sage lingered in the air. Sage grew everywhere on the reservation, and the Navajo used it to cleanse and purify a room before engaging in a ceremony or an important meeting. The men in attendance all sat together at the front of the room. The women huddled together at the back. Not sure where to sit, Terry and I took seats in the middle of the room. Pamela, our NPS Liaison, had come with us and would answer any questions regarding National Park Service polices and regulations involving SJM. She would also help with the interpreting.

The Navajo Council delegate from Oljato, *Hastiin* Walter Ateen, called the chapter meeting to order. Walter was a very slim man and stood about five feet tall. His white, straw cowboy hat, however, made him appear taller. He wore a red and gray plaid western long-sleeved shirt, and jeans that fit closely to his thin legs. His posture was so straight that it looked like he had shoulder pads in his shirts. He stood with his thumbs in his jean pockets. The corners of his smiling eyes turned up behind wire rimmed glasses, and a thin black mustache grew above his thin lips. His soft voice could easily be heard throughout the room as he spoke. The meeting began and all business was done in proper parliamentary procedure. Because Terry and I were present, each sentence was translated into English so we would not feel left out. After the minutes and the old business were read, reviewed and passed upon, new business was introduced. After several different business matters were brought to attention, examined and voted upon, it was time for SJM to be discussed. Terry was asked to come forward. As he did, I noticed his legs appeared a little shaky, and I knew how very nervous he must have been. He wanted to make a good impression and project the most positive attitude he could for SJM and its employees. He smiled and began to speak in a calm low voice.

"How very proud you should all be of your children," he said. "They are some of the most hardworking and loyal employees I have ever had the pleasure of working with." He stopped between thoughts so that the interpretation could be made and then he proceeded. He explained the training program that was ongoing and how the marina was providing jobs for their children as well as much needed revenues for the community. He encouraged them to not believe any rumors but to listen to their children and what truths they told. He invited everyone to come out to the marina and see what was really happening there. He assured them that it was his intention, as the leader of the marina, to follow their wishes and ban the use of alcohol. Nor would mischief be tolerated. Continuing, he gave a financial report and reviewed the future plans for the marina. It was now time for a question and answer session. It was very interesting to watch and listen as Terry and the interpreter patiently took turns speaking. Everyone's attention focused upon Terry as he answered all their questions with confidence and sincerity. I was filled with much pride and admiration for him that day. I could see he had already won over the crowd.

Two hours had passed before it appeared that everyone was through asking questions. As the momentum slowed, *Hastiin* Fatt rose and walked to the front of the building. Voices fell silent as he prepared to speak. Jim was known by everyone in this community to have the final say on any matter discussed. He carried a lot of clout among his peers as his opinion was highly respected. To us, Jim Fatt epitomized the appearance of how a classic Native American Indian should look. His face stern and unsmiling, Jim gave the appearance that he would be a hard nut to crack. He began to make an emphatic sounding speech using many hand gestures and pursing his lips. We held our breath waiting for him to finish so we could hear the translation and see if we had won the favor of this community. As he finished, he looked at Terry and me and smiled. He placed his right hand over his heart and nodded. Even before the translation began we knew he was on our side and we immediately fell in love with him.

As the meeting adjourned and we rose to leave, everyone clapped. We were invited to share coffee and homemade cupcakes. Even though our ability to communicate in Navajo was very limited, we had a good time shaking hands and receiving warm looks of welcome. Terry and I felt as if a major milestone had been passed, and that SJM could now truly be a beacon for this Navajo community. We had their support. Now the rumors could stop.

SEPTEMBER 22 – 30

Living and working at a marina provides one with some perks. Employees were entitled to use the houseboats, cost free, if there was availability. Of course, the customer always came first. But as the visitation to Lake Powell and SJM began to slow down after Labor Day, houseboats became available for employee enjoyment. Terry and I took one of our fifty-foot houseboats out for a one-week mini vacation. It was our busman's holiday as we took time to explore the San Juan River and enjoy the sights just like any regular customer. Also, we had invited several relatives and friends to join us. Many of our friends brought their own houseboats, and before long we had a regular armada floating down the San Juan River. We anchored on a large sandbar in Naskahie Bay, a wide, deep and popular camping spot that was surrounded by towering canyon walls. Tables were set upon the beach, and in the evenings laughter filled the air as we devoured delicious pitch-in meals. Campfires were a nightly ritual with marshmallows to roast. Guitar playing and singing could be heard late into the nights. Days were filled with swimming, fishing, water skiing and exploring more of the San Juan. Everyone was excited about the project at SJM and wanted to hear all about it. Our family and friends came to realize how important our lives with our Navajo employees and the success of SJM had become to us. Many of our friends decided to visit the marina and see why we appeared to be so happy. Their interest gave us encouragement and the praises that they gave after visiting the marina were uplifting.

CHAPTER FIVE
October 1987
Good Morning America

OCTOBER 1

Today we received an unwelcome surprise. Two gentlemen representing the First Western Bank of Salt Lake City came to the marina. They informed us that our houseboats were about to be repossessed. Our jaws dropped open in shock. Upon further investigation, we found out that our boss had taken out a loan for over $600,000 one year ago to purchase our houseboats. That note was due today. But apparently not one penny of the loan had been repaid to the bank. The only thing we could do was to refer the men to Mr. K at his office in Albuquerque, New Mexico. After the men left, Terry and I agreed that "Something is rotten in the state of Denmark," as they say. Many questions began popping into our minds. From now on, we agreed to keep our eyes and ears open and start making notation of all unusual events. We had no idea that this was just the tip of the iceberg.

OCTOBER 2 – 7

Get your cameras ready! Six months before SJM was to open, the Navajo Nation advertised the marina through newspaper articles, radio announcements and a brochure, co-published with Goulding's Trading Post, which showcased the Monument Valley area. A central reservations office was set up in Blanding, Utah, and the public was given a phone number to call to make their houseboat rental reservations. But now it was time to teach our employees how to market and advertise the marina themselves. We would start by designing our own brochures. The kids were very excited. Many hours were spent taking pictures and getting them developed. The pictures that we were going to use in our new brochures had to be just right. The kids had many creative ideas about the brochure layout, and they were involved with it from start to finish. They learned about selecting and dealing with a printing company and how to anticipate and budget for the costs. After a month of hard work, the brochures were ready to send to the printers. They turned out to be very eye-catching and our kids puffed up with pride when they saw them. We complimented them highly on this successful accomplishment by putting "designed by employees of SJM" on the backs of the brochures. Now it was time to learn about distribution.

There were several methods we used to advertise SJM. First, we decided to invite several journalists and sports writers to experience a houseboat vacation first hand so they could write about their adventure. Their articles would appear in many publications throughout our intended marketing areas. One such publication was The Grand Circle Adventure. It advertised an area referred to as the Grand Circle, which included Lake Powell, Monument Valley, Bryce and Zion national parks. This publication reached thousands and thousands of readers who were potential houseboat customers. So we sent invitations to thirty writers. They were invited to be our guests at a slide presentation at Goulding's Trading Post with entertainment and food provided afterward.

Sandy, our Boat Reservation Coordinator, was chosen to make the slide presentation. She and I wrote a script to accompany the slides, and we practiced and practiced until it was memorized. Terry would also be available to make introductions and help with answering questions regarding SJM.

Most of those present had heard about SJM and eagerly

accepted our invitation to the slide presentation. The offer of a free houseboat trip and an invitation to write about it were alluring. We all gathered in the old Goulding house at the trading post to watch the presentation. Sandy and I grew nervous as we dimmed the lights to show our slides. Her voice was a little unsteady at first, but as she hit her stride, she gained her confidence. She did an excellent job. Everyone was excited that the San Juan River and Lake Powell could now be easily accessed by going to SJM, and each writer was now eager to tell his or her readers about it. After the question and answer period was completed and our new brochures had been passed out, Sandy, Terry and I heaved a great sigh of relief. SJM had claimed its place on the map and we could go eat.

The sun had already slipped behind the well-known Monument Valley sandstone formations of the Bear and Rabbit as we rode in an old buckboard wagon out into the Navajo desert. The evening sky was turning shades of dark blue and red-violet with pink and yellow-orange streaks across it. The warm breeze hugged our shoulders and the smell of sagebrush and pinyon filled the night air. Arriving at a chuck wagon near a glowing campfire, we could smell the aroma of fresh brewing coffee and food. Two local cowboy guitar pickers were strumming familiar country tunes, which made one want to tap one's feet. After eating a hearty meal of grilled steaks, fried potatoes and cowboy beans, we finished off with homemade cherry pie. We gathered around the campfire, sipped our coffee and sang along with our newest friends. What a wonderful evening it turned out to be. In this setting we felt as if time had stopped.

OCTOBER 8 – 14

Most people in the Anglo world hurry from day to day trying to beat the clock. Our lives have become consumed with trying to see how many activities we can cram into a twenty-four hour day. We have actually become slaves to our watches, phones, and schedules. Time seems to rule our lives. In the Navajo culture the concept of time has an entirely different meaning. When we lived at SJM, Terry and I had to understand their concept of time and accept it so we would not have nervous breakdowns, conniption fits and ulcers. We had to throw our watches away. Let me tell you why.

There appears to be several reasons why most Navajo have a relaxed attitude toward the concept of time. They have lived on a farmer's clock, residing in remote areas, farming and tending livestock. No industries have provided jobs that needed people to clock in and out each day. No one had to be at any certain place on any certain day at any certain time. In addition, their required attendance at ceremonies does not allow for any loyalties toward time constrictions. If a ceremony is announced, all of the immediate family and its extended clan members are expected to attend. Not to attend a ceremony is considered an insult that is beyond repair. No matter how far one has to travel or how much it costs or if one has a job or not, one must attend the ceremony he or she has been invited to. Family ties and obligations and cultural etiquette take precedence over everything.

Ceremonies can last anywhere from a few hours to nine full days and nights. Terry and I quickly learned that Anglo business rules of job attendance simply did not always apply at SJM. First of all, none of our employees had telephones to notify us of their planned or unplanned absences from work. When an employee did not show up for work for several days or even a week, we learned not to be too alarmed. The absences were not necessarily a cause for the employee's dismissal from his or her job. We discovered that the employees who did show up for work did not seem to mind that their counterparts were absent, and they gladly took up the slack so the work could get done. No one complained because they knew their fellow employees would do the same for them. If an employee arrived late for work, he stayed until the job was finished. It was more important to finish a project, not to see how fast it could be done. Terry and I guessed that this was one reason fate had chosen us for this task. Most of the Anglos we knew could not have functioned within the Navajo viewpoint of time. We had no choice but to accept it, and actually this helped us enjoy a more stress -free way of life. So much for wearing watches.

OCTOBER 15 – 21

We are going to be on TV! Yesterday, we received word that Good Morning America, the well known national TV show, would be sending film crews to Monument Valley to journalize a story about the Navajo people who lived there. SJM is to be included in that documentary.

Needless to say, we were all very, very excited. Although a little nervous, our employees were thrilled to be able to show off all the efforts they had put into their marina. Everyone worked hard to give the marina a good scrubbing and polishing. The kids had smiling faces and they chattered and laughed among themselves, as they got ready for the big event. To tell the truth, Terry and I were quite anxious but thoroughly delighted to have this opportunity to show SJM to the world. More importantly it would demonstrate how the Navajo could compete within the Anglo world of economic development. Of course, the national exposure wouldn't hurt our business any.

The day arrived that the film crews were expected. Our employees showed up for work wearing their employee shirts starched and pressed. Pride and anticipation were evident on their faces. We were all so happy.

Well, we waited and waited. And we waited some more. Afternoon approached and still no one came. As dusk began to descend upon us, we wondered if a cruel joke had been played on us. We were in total disbelief. Good Morning America did not come.

You can only begin to imagine what a disappointed group of employees we had. Their smiles had turned into puzzled and disappointed frowns. Their shoulders slumped, and they quietly left the marina to return to their homes. Terry and I had no words to comfort them. We didn't know what had happened and had not received any communication from our boss.

Well, the next day word came that the Good Morning America crews had indeed come to the Monument Valley area to film. But apparently they did not have the time for us. We guessed that someone just didn't think our story was important, and the twenty-nine miles were just too far to drive to film us and get our story. The words of some Anglos could not apparently be trusted any better now than in the old days.

We had to try to lift the spirits of our kids. So Terry and I planned an awards banquet to be held right away. We all met at the Goulding's restaurant and we ate as many of the barbecued ribs we could hold. Restoring their self-esteem was more important to us that any TV show promotion, and we wanted to bolster their self-esteem. Each employee was presented with a gimmick award that fit his or her job description. For example, the plumber was given a toilet plunger as his award. The truck drivers were given toy trucks as their awards. So on and so forth it went until everyone received an award. Terry and I made up little rhymes for each employee as they received their awards. Before long, everyone was laughing and having a good time. By the end of the evening, it was apparent that they were feeling much better about thewhole situation. Their humor returned and they jokingly said that Good Morning America should change their story. Instead of reporting on how the Navajo lived, they should report on how the Navajo had gotten screwed by a white man again. Some things never change, it seems.

All of the electricity used at SJM was created and distributed from two diesel-powered generators. Daily maintenance of the generators was one of the most important jobs at the marina. If the generator went down, our entire marina operations were at risk. Oil levels had to be checked and maintained daily. The batteries had to be checked, cleaned, refilled with water and watched closely for potential problems. Also, we had a maintenance agreement that called for a monthly inspection of the generators by the company where we had bought them. This week the generator mechanics had come to check and service the generators. They had reported that everything was working well. Then they had left.

It was late the next night when we woke from our sleep and realized that our mobile home had no heat. Our furnace was not running. We had no electricity. We could not hear the generators making their normally loud and steady humming sound. What had happened? What if we had to replace the generators? Since most of the employees that lived on the marina compound were on their days off and were not on site, Terry and I were the only ones available to investigate the problem. We took a flashlight and went to the generators. There were no stars in the sky and the blackness seemed to close in around us as we tried to see what had happened. There we were standing in our nightclothes, the wind howling and blowing. Fine sand stung our bodies and swirled around us getting into our hair, mouths and eyes. Terry discovered that the generator batteries were dead. They had been allowed to boil themselves dry. Had not the mechanics just been at the marina the day before and said everything was all right? There was nothing to do but try to get new batteries. Terry had to drive ninety miles one-way, to a store that he knew was open all night, to buy the new batteries. As I sat alone in the candle-lit darkness of my home listening to the forlorn sound of the howling wind, I wondered if all the effort we had put into the marina was worth it. No one would ever believe how challenging it was to live here. After about three hours, Terry returned and I helped him lift the 150-pound batteries into position in the generator. Terry filled the oil chambers with oil and we used our truck to jumpstart the batteries. Obediently the generators took off and another problem had been solved. At least we would never ever run out of stories to tell our grandchildren.

OCTOBER 31

Today was Halloween. Our workload had slowed down and the weather had become cold and rainy. We were all quitting work early to prepare for SJM's first Halloween party. Even though Halloween did not have any roots in Navajo tradition it was observed by most. And it meant a way to get all the candy one wanted. The employees came with their children and their extended family members. Most of the children were dressed in costumes. Some were dressed in store- bought costumes portraying popular characters like a princess or a super hero. Other children wore masks over their faces, and one child just wore a large plain brown paper bag over his head with two cut out holes in it to see through. They all brought large bags and/or pillowcases to collect the anticipated gifts of candy. We popped corn, made donuts from canned biscuits, and dipped apples into melted caramel. I dressed like a witch complete with a black pointed hat and a wart on my nose. I served my famous "witches' brew" (a very tasty spicy apple cider punch) and passed out lots of candy. We played games, bobbed for apples and cut out faces on pumpkins. It was the best Halloween party we had ever attended.

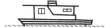

CHAPTER SIX
November 1987
Our Basketball Team

Terry left today for Denver, Colorado. He took three of our mechanics (Todd, Clifford and Fred) to attend Outboard Motor Mechanic School. The NPS required that all mechanics working at marinas on Lake Powell have outboard motor certification. The only way to get certified was to attend a qualified outboard motor repair school. The closest school to SJM was located in Denver. These three employees had never traveled far from their homes and had never been to Colorado. They were excited not only to have the opportunity to see new places but to be able to get more education. The school would last five days and Terry was counting on full cooperation from the guys to work hard and to pass the classes. He had his fingers crossed that while they were in Denver the guys wouldn't get into any mischief. Clifford, Todd and Fred were known as the three musketeers of devilment. Numerous tales of their pranks and horseplay had provided us all with many hours of laughter at the marina. However, this school was not the place to display their antics.

Fred had been raised alongside of Todd and Clifford. All three had gone to school together and had been good friends for all of their lives. They were all mechanics of one kind or another. Todd was the oldest of the three and had been a car mechanic for most of his adult life. He had graying hair at his temples and was on the stout side. He never said much and was a steady worker. He usually stood with his hands in his pockets and looked around on the ground as if he were searching for something, even when he talked to you. Todd did, however, have a temper, especially when provoked by Fred or Clifford. He was usually at the heart of a prank and enjoyed a good laugh, especially if it was at Fred's or Clifford's expense. Clifford was a tall lean muscle machine. He had a bristle brush mustache and always wore a black baseball cap. He was our nonconformist and didn't mind letting us know how he felt about things. He loved to roughhouse whenever the opportunity provided itself, especially with Todd and Fred. Most of all, Clifford loved his big black four-wheel drive pickup truck with large oversized tires. If he wasn't working, he was in his truck. It usually had red Navajo mud caked on it as Clifford loved to mud bog.

The outboard motor school started off well and the boys studied hard. They wanted Terry to be proud of them and they wanted those certificates very badly. At the end of the classes there was a test to be passed to obtain certification. Todd, Clifford and Fred were very nervous as they went to the final class for the test. Afterwards, they waited with anticipation to see the posted grades. They had all studied hard and had behaved like perfect gentlemen. As they huddled around the bulletin board that held the final scores, Terry held his breath. When each saw his name with the passing grade behind it, an old-fashioned Indian war whoop was released. They had all passed with high marks.

Now they could celebrate. Terry took the guys out to the nicest restaurant he could find and bought them anything they wanted to eat. Afterward they attended a movie. On the way back to their hotel rooms, Terry expressed his pride and gratitude to them and then he went on to retire to his own room, telling the boys that they should be ready to leave Denver about 8 a.m. the next morning and that they would stop for breakfast on the way home.

The next morning when it was past the time to start for home, Terry went to the boys' room to see if they were ready to leave. He knocked on the door. No answer. He knocked again. There was still no answer. After more and much louder knocking, the door slowly opened and Fred stood in front of him, yawning and scratching his tousled hair. Terry could see that Todd and Clifford were still asleep. All three still had their clothes on from the night before. Terry concluded that the constraint of holding back all their natural playfulness had gotten the best of them. They had probably given into their natural feelings of adventure and had decided to go out on the town after Terry had left to go to his room for the night.

Well, to this day, it is still not known just how those three guys did their celebrating, but at least there were no warrants out for their arrest. The trip home was quiet, as Terry did not want to ask any questions. The boys had done a good job and what mattered was that he was very proud of them.

NOVEMBER 8 – 14

Job layoffs were never welcomed or easy to give. Especially when the employees had given one hundred percent of themselves and had performed their jobs well. Also, it was very difficult to explain to someone who spoke limited English just why he or she couldn't retain a much-needed job. Our business was slowing and revenues were decreasing. Payroll expenses could be lowered with a few layoffs and financially the marina could get through the winter. But which employees would be laid off?

Terry's kindhearted nature would be put to the test. He didn't want our kids to misunderstand the motives for the layoffs or feel that he might be favoring one employee over another. They had all done their jobs well. We had told them so many times. Would they think we didn't value them? Would they distinguish between common business sense and our personal inclinations?

Terry agonized over the decisions he had to make. Well, it must be done. So he called all the employees together to explain the situation. As he spoke, he watched the emotions showing on their faces. Brows wrinkled, eyes looked from one to another and then were cast downward. One could cut the silence with a knife. He continued as he was even more determined to make them understand. Next he named the employees that were to be laid off. When no one offered comment or question, Terry reluctantly dismissed the meeting. It was done.

The next day one of the employees, Iris, who had been laid off, gave us a letter. It had been written for her as she could not write or speak English. Iris was a little older than most of our women employees. She always wore a sweet soft smile that accompanied a timid look as she would slightly bow her head and look up with her large brown eyes. She was a tiny woman, just under five feet tall. She wasn't thin but not fat either. Her voice was so soft that you had to strain to hear it. She was a very hard worker and one of the best houseboat maids we had. After reading the letter, tears came to our eyes. It was apparent that she did understand about our plight regarding the layoffs and she wanted us to know that she did not blame us personally.

To this day, our hearts fill with humility and tears come to our eyes each time we read this letter. Iris also gave us a gift of a horse blanket that she had made. Not only had she sheared the sheep by hand, she also hand combed and dyed the wool. She then hand spun the wool into strands and wove them into a blanket. One can scarcely begin to understand what a personal gesture of love this meant to us. We proudly and lovingly displayed that rug along with the many other gifts that we received from our employees while living at SJM. We cherished her gift dearly.

We were going to attend live theater, Navajo style. A dance company named Lamanite Generation was going to perform at the Monument Valley High School. The dance company consisted of college students from many different tribes from many different parts of the world. This was one of the few formal events of the year that we had been invited to attend. Terry and I dressed up in our best western clothes including hats and boots. We wore all the turquoise we owned and we practiced all the Navajo words we knew.

We entered the high school auditorium and took seats among some of our employees and their families. As the lights dimmed and the music started, we felt excitement in the air. The dancers came on stage, one by one, dressed in their native costumes. The Hawaiian Islands, the Philippines, Eskimos, and many other tribes of the North and South Americas were represented. Many of the brightly colored costumes were made of animal skins, furs, feathers and tropical leaves. They were then adorned with fringe, beads, animal teeth and claws. Drums beat loudly to the rhythms of the different songs and dances. The dancers moved and jumped to the beat of the drums. The performance held our attention with a hypnotic effect. The narrative that accompanied the entertainment was educational, giving a welcomed insight into the many original cultures from all over the world. It was an impressive performance.

As we sat quietly in the darkened auditorium, we felt the sensation that we had become part of something very meaningful and significant; not the show, but the people we were sitting among. Looking around at the dimly lit faces that surrounded us, we saw how happiness was reflected in their smiles and their eyes. Their reddish-brown skin glistened and emphasized their hard-earned wrinkles; the result of years of living hard lives and surviving difficult conditions. Each person looked relaxed, calm and content. We watched the children as they sat on the edge of their seats giving full attention to the dancers. They clapped and laughed with delight. Terry and I smiled at each other, and we felt a warm inward glow that made our souls feel like they were soaring. Again, like many other times while living among the Navajo, we felt as if time had stopped. Was this what our friends meant by living in harmony?

After the show was over, the audience was invited to share in refreshments. By now we knew many of the community residents by sight and name. So, as we took our place among the crowd, we greeted and shook hands with many of our new friends. We had mastered numerous Navajo words and could exchange the basic pleasantries without making too many pronunciation errors. We felt humbled and slightly embarrassed as we seemed to be receiving more attention than the dance company.

NOVEMBER 22 – 28

Thanksgiving Day fell on the twenty-sixth this year. Since the marina would be closed to observe the holiday, most of our employees planned to spend it with their families. To show our appreciation and give our kids a taste of a midwestern -style Thanksgiving Day dinner, we invited everyone for a family feast. One thing I had learned early on at SJM was that food was always taken in large amounts, and it was customary for any leftovers to be divided among the guests and to be taken home. One had better prepare for many hungry mouths.

For this Thanksgiving dinner, I roasted two twenty-four-pound turkeys and baked two fifteen-pound hams. I prepared six batches of homemade noodles and four large pans each of dressing and mashed potatoes. In addition to the two gallons of giblet gravy, the traditional green bean casserole, and marshmallow-covered yams, we prepared several Jell-O salads. A dozen pies made of pumpkin, apple and cherry topped off the traditional foods that we wanted to share. When the food was ready, our guests began to arrive to help devour our feast. After a couple of hours, our bellies were full and we finished the day with coffee and conversation. After dividing up the leftover food, our guests began to leave. It had turned out to be a wonderful Thanksgiving Day and we knew we really had a lot to be thankful for.

NOVEMBER 29 – 30

We had our own basketball team at SJM. The San Juan Lakers, as we called ourselves, were made up of all of our male employees. There had been enough money in the budget to purchase new basketball jerseys, new tennis shoes and even an official NBA basketball for our team. There was nothing that our Navajo kids liked to do better than to play basketball. Terry had been chosen as the coach, and we women went to the games to cheer for our team.

Now, Terry had been a good high school basketball player when he played in the fifties and sixties. He had been a terrific left-handed basketball dribbler and knew the rules of defensive play well. His high school coach had always instructed his players to hold their hands up and guard their man, one on one. But it became apparent, very quickly I might add, that Navajo basketball of the eighties was played very differently. They played a fast paced, run, pass and shoot game. The kids played with a very competitive spirit, and it appeared that they literally tried to kill each other on the basketball court.

Terry could not understand why the team kept running and shooting the ball and paid no attention to defense. Finally, he put himself into the game to show the kids how to play proper Anglo basketball. It was clear that those kids were too energetic for him and it wasn't long until he was pooped. He did, however, manage to get a broken finger, several broken ribs and a technical foul before the evening was over. That night he was not the boss. He had become an equal. After that episode he just coached from the sidelines. Our team lost their first game, but took first place at the end of the season. Everyone had a marvelous time and our team even got a great big trophy.

CHAPTER SEVEN
December 1987
Skin Walkers and Murder

DECEMBER 4

Many Navajo beliefs, stories and traditions have survived since the beginning of their creation. Those beliefs are just as real to the Navajo today as they were to their ancestors. One such belief is the existence of the Skin Walker. It is an interesting and somewhat controversial viewpoint that many still debate to this day. Is the skin walker a myth, folklore, a scary bedtime story, a Halloween ghost tale, a natural phenomenon or the real thing?

It is believed that a person who had turned evil, by his own desires or by a sickness beyond his control, could become a ghost and inflict harm upon others. The witch could then take the form of a coyote, or that of a half-man/half-coyote and stand up on two legs. Upon observation, the witch might look like a bare-chested man walking upright with a coyote skin thrown over his head and back; thus the term Skin Walker. In this form, he could move so fast and could change form so quickly that one wondered if they had really seen something or not. The sighting of a skin walker meant that something very evil and dreadful was about to happen. Was the witch giving its victim a chance to prepare for its fate? Or could it be a vision or a telepathic way to prevent future events? Who can say?

Terry and I had been gone from the marina for a few days and it was late afternoon when we started our drive back home. The sky was overcast with the dark clouds indicating an approaching storm. As we drove on, the night darkness fell fast. Rain started falling as we continued on our way across the empty desert. Suddenly, lightning began striking and loud thunder accompanied each bolt. That eerie blue light, that lighting makes, made the shadows from the rocks and sagebrush along the side of the road seem larger than they were and very foreboding. It was now raining very heavily. Uneasy and unexplained feelings of fear began to wash over our souls and we both expressed our impatience to get home.

Suddenly, an extremely large lightening bolt struck near the passenger side of our car. As we looked out we saw a tall human form wearing what appeared to be a long black coat or cape, stand up behind a nearby bush and bolt quickly away and disappear. What was that running after the man? Was it a large dog? But who would be out here on foot this time of night? We were miles from town and we had seen no cars, no houses and no lights. Why would the man disappear? Did he need help? We slowed the car and honked the horn and strained to see if we could see someone or something. We looked at each other and knew we were reading each other's thoughts. We knew we had both seen something but couldn't explain what.

The storm grew in intensity. The lightening worsened and the thunder grew louder. We were driving through hard-hitting rain now and the wind was gusting with great force. We finally arrived at home and quickly went inside. The electricity was out so we went to bed. It was approximately 10 p.m.

Long into the night, we were both suddenly and literally shaken out of our bed by one enormously loud thunderclap. The brightest lightning we had ever seen was all around us. The wind was howling fiercely. Suddenly it all stopped and it was quiet. Nothing stirred. There was a deafening silence: no wind, no thunder, no lightening and no rain. We stood by our bedroom window looking out into the darkness, stunned and a little shaken. After a short time had passed we calmed down and returned to our bed and gradually fell back to sleep. Was Mother Nature trying to alert us to something?

DECEMBER 5

The next morning we were starting our daily duties of opening the marina when a local Navajo man came running into the store. He had a wide–eyed expression and he spoke loudly and rapidly, waving his hands and pointing toward the road. It was clear he was very upset. All of our employees gathered around him to hear his story. After waiting for the interpretation, we learned that this man had been on his way to go fishing when he came upon a startling sight. He reported seeing two half burned Navajo police vans still smoldering. He had looked inside one of the vans and had seen what appeared to be two partially burned bodies. The vans were stuck in the mud by Copper Canyon Road which veered off from our SJM road about seven miles away. Someone ran and fetched our NPS Ranger, who immediately called the NPS dispatch and the Navajo Police. He then went out to investigate.

What he found was horrible. The partially charred bodies of two Navajo policemen were found in the back of one of the burned vans. They appeared to be policemen whom we all knew and who had regularly looked after our marina. This event turned our Navajo community inside out during the days, weeks and months that followed. We remember it all too well the sadness and horror when we do. It was after this event that Terry and I learned of the Skin Walker theory. Had we actually seen one that night before the crimes has been committed?

The Navajo view of death, and how they deal with it, is different to the various Anglo perceptions of it. The names of the dead are never spoken so, in deference to their tradition, we will not mention by name the police officers that were killed. The concept of death itself was never discussed with us but our understanding is that their dead do go on to an afterworld, and it is important for the funeral to occur as soon as possible after death. The funeral rites must be performed carefully for, if they are not done properly, the ghost of the dead will not leave this world but will haunt it. Terry and I understood that a nine-day ceremony followed any death and that all of the families and clan related families were required to attend. During the ceremony the families buried the loved one, prayed for the spirit of the dead's journey and also prayed for all living family members. It was a time for the families of the deceased to grieve and to gain support from their family and friends.

Most of our employees were related to the officers in one way or another, so Terry and I were left to man the marina by ourselves for many days.

DECEMBER 6 – 8

Since the crime occurred on United States Federal Land, the Navajo Reservation, and the State of Utah and in the county of San Juan, there were many different law enforcement agencies that became involved in the investigation. The FBI, the Navajo Police, men from the Bureau of Indian Affairs, State and County policemen and Federal Marshals flooded the Monument Valley area. Hundreds of people in uniforms or black suits were everywhere.

Our NPS Ranger, Gary, provided help with the Navajo language translation and interpretation. He was a very handsome Navajo man who appeared to be middle aged. He always looked very well groomed and official in his Ranger uniform. His pleasant, quiet, and polite demeanor was the first thing that you noticed about Gary. His knowledge and the way he articulated his language when doing his job gave you the impressions that he knew his job well. Gary had been a NPS Ranger for many years but never had he seen such a terrible homicide. The fact that this tragedy happened, not only to fellow officers, but also to fellow Navajo, really gave Gary an uneasy feeling. Months later, after the investigation was completed, Gary decided to move from SJM and eventually retired from the NPS. Presently, though, everyone involved with the case wanted to get to the bottom of this sickening crime. Someone had to pay. Our peaceful and quiet little community was in shock. Who could have done such a deed and why? We were frightened and scared that the killer or killers, who were still unaccounted for, might strike again. Our days and especially our nights remained restless for many weeks ahead. With the law enforcement came the media and the curiosity seekers. It was hard for Terry and me and our employees to keep our minds on our business. We still had a marina to run and customers to serve. Over the long days, weeks, and months of intense investigation, the tragic story was eventually pieced together. Matters only got worse for us when two suspects were taken into custody and one of the alleged killers was one of our own employees. We were stunned and, to this day, we don't believe it.

After concluding their investigations, the FBI described how they thought the crime took place. Early in the evening of December 4th, a campfire party was being held in one of the often visited but more secluded areas near Monument Valley. Apparently twenty to thirty high school kids were attending the party. We think maybe a few familiar or unfamiliar faces of strangers were there too. As the evening progressed, someone brought beer and, possibly, drugs to the party. After a while several kids had become intoxicated and high. (Alcohol and drugs are illegal on the Navajo Reservation but most of the kids know where to get them.) There was always plenty of booze or pills at these parties. Of course, no one would ever tell where or from whom the alcohol or drugs had come. Everyone who attended these parties knew that before the evening was over, the two well known Navajo Police officers would probably be showing up to break up the party.

This had happened many times before and the kids all knew the routine. The two officers would wait until the kids had had a little fun, and then they would show up and break up the party and see to it that everyone got home safely. The policemen were always in radio contact, if not actually together, when doing their patrols. Apparently, one of the officers had decided to patrol the area where the party was happening by himself. He had radioed to his partner and said he would "check out the party and see how everything was going." If he needed help he would radio back to the second officer for assistance.

No one knew for sure (or at least they would not say) but it appeared that the first officer met resistance from someone when he arrived at the party. He did not have time to radio for help from his partner before his gun was taken away from him. He was apparently quickly and severely beaten and several teeth were even knocked out. He was wounded with his own gun and became unconscious. His hands were held together behind his back with his own handcuffs. After about an hour, the second officer became suspicious when he had not heard from his partner. He drove over where the party was being held and was soon apprehended by the same people and met with the same fate as the first officer. The attacks appeared to be well planned and well organized. Witnesses told investigators that both men were still alive at this point. Yes, there were many witnesses! Everyone at the party knew what had happened, but no one was going to tell. It was suspected that whoever did the killing threatened the witnesses with their lives if they were revealed. A good Navajo knew when to keep his or her mouth shut. The witnesses had many extended family members who lived in the Monument Valley area and the attackers evidently knew this and had the manpower and the guns to enforce their threats.

The attackers put the two wounded policemen in the caged area in the back of their own police Suburban vehicles.

Evidently reluctant drivers, threatened by guns and death, drove the vans out toward Copper Canyon on the San Juan Road. Apparently the killers were trying to get the vans to the San Juan River where they could be driven into the water and the evidence could be hidden. However, the storms had started and when the rains worsened, the roads got very slick and the vans became stuck in the mud. When the attackers saw that they could not get the vans unstuck, they decided to set them on fire. The vans were still smoldering when they were discovered the next morning.

Now, everyone had their own opinions and theories about why and how these two murders were committed. And, yes, we had ours. First of all, most Navajo do not believe in burning a human body. It is taboo and not associated with their beliefs. Secondly, most Navajo never carry any extra gasoline with them. Thirdly, the Navajo might have disagreements among themselves but would never murder anyone on purpose. Murder would disrupt the harmony by which the Navajo lives his or her life. Maybe there were drug dealers, non-Navajo, at that party that had a lot of firepower. Maybe these people had the power to carry out their threats to those who attended the party. The killers seemed to know that if these Navajo were scared enough, they would not talk. No one will ever know because no one will ever talk about what really happened that night. But someone out there knows the truth.

DECEMBER 9 – 12

The two murdered policemen were young men who left behind wives and children. During the weeks that followed, there were many memorial services held in our local community, other nearby communities and even at the Navajo Nation's capital, Window Rock, for the slain policemen. Many bank accounts were set up to take in donations, which would help provide for the wives and children of the murdered men. Our community tried to get back to its daily routine of living. But it was hard. It seemed as if the gossip and the rumors would never stop. We had all been questioned and interviewed by many of the investigators, and we had been told not to discuss those interviews with anyone. But it seemed the investigations would go on forever. There were too many footprints and tire tracks at the place where the burned vans were found, and there were no clear clues found at the party site. There was very little cooperation among the witnesses and their families as they refused to talk about anything to the investigators. Everyone seemed to be scared. Why wouldn't the witnesses speak up? The events that had occurred were never far from our minds. But because of the instructions of the investigators, and the Navajo beliefs concerning the dead, not much was said among our employees to each other or us. Our moods were solemn and sad, and we didn't know how to comfort each other.

The weather began to turn colder and the winter skies were cloudy and gray. The wind seemed to share and enhance our feelings as it howled for days on end. The water around the marina was choppy and the white caps caused from the force of the wind made boating and fishing difficult. Our emotions had started with shock, stayed at disbelief and grief for a while, and then proceeded on to constant sadness. We heard that several healing ceremonies were being held around the neighborhood, but we never had the courage to ask who had attended. We sure needed something good to come along to help us get through this troubled time.

DECEMBER 13 – 18

Well, something did come along to ease our minds from these events. There appeared to be brighter days ahead. We had been invited to participate in the annual Lake Powell Parade of Lights competition. It would be held at Bullfrog Marina about 100 miles up lake from SJM. We had only a few days to come up with a theme and then decorate our entry, a fifty-foot house-boat. Our employees worked feverishly to put their ideas into effect. Over fifty sets of Christmas lights were purchased, and the kids designed and made all of the other decorations. The houseboat was to depict Navajo life in Monument Valley. The kids used papier-mâché, chicken wire and PVC pipe to construct a replica of the famous rock formations known as the Mittens in Monument Valley. They placed that on top of the houseboat. They made a hogan scaled to the size of the rocks and placed it near the formations with faux smoke coming from the smoke hole in the top. A large (ten feet in diameter) duplication of a Navajo wedding basket was drawn on white sheets and tightly stretched across PVC pipe. It was placed in front of the back door of the houseboat. It also had lights all round it to show off the detail of its design. Lights were also placed around all the windows and front doors. The words "*Merry Késhmısh*" (a Navajo Merry Christmas) were spelled out in lights along each side of the houseboat and the employees who went with the boat wore traditional Navajo costumes. The boats were to be judged on how they looked in the daylight as well as the nighttime. Terry and I were unable to go with the boat as other duties called, but we had eight of our employees go with the boat. And guess what: our houseboat took first place! The kids were thrilled and of course we were exceptionally happy that they had beat out all of the other entries from the other marinas on the lake. The kids presented Terry and me with the trophy they had won because they said, "You had faith in us."

DECEMBER 19 – 23

It had started to snow. It snowed and snowed and then snowed some more. Within a few days we had eight to ten inches of new snow everywhere around the area. What a beautiful picture it made! The white snow was piled high on top of the red cliffs and rust colored sandstone hills like icing on a cake.

The green trees scattered among the copper colored rocks on the tall mesas looked as if someone had dusted them with powered sugar. Mother Earth was quiet and looked like she was resting with a great white shawl around her shoulders.

But life at San Juan Marina was not resting. We still had to haul water into the marina compound every day to exist. So, when the employees went out to get the water they discovered that the water spigot had broken off and the water in the underground pipe was frozen solid. There was no water to get. So Terry and several of the boys took shovels and picks and went where the frozen pipe was (about fourteen miles away) and tried to dig it up and thaw it out. Sheep, cattle and horses constantly grazed in the field where we got our water, and the animals were always knocking off the top of the pipe. To fix the pipe was not a problem when the ground wasn't frozen, but now the story was different. The ground around the pipe was frozen solid, too. Apparently, there hadn't been a winter as cold as this one for many, many years. Would we be without water until spring?

The next day several of the employees again went out to try to dig out the frozen water pipe, thaw it out, and repair it. A backhoe would be required for this job, so off they went to find one. George was our large equipment operator. He drove the diesel truck most of the time and operated the backhoe. George was of average build. He wore his black, shoulder-length hair straight or pulled back into a ponytail. He was very solemn and quiet, and it was easy to overlook his presence. He hung in the background of the other employees but always kept busy working. He was a very hard worker. So it was George that took the backhoe out to help repair the water leak. After a deep trench had been dug, the men thawed out the water, put the pipe into it and covered it up so that it would not freeze up again. When it was all said and done we were only without water for two days. Not bad for us. This was another temporary utility project that

The marina store is the building on the left

Houseboats moored at the floating dock

*The dreaded
orange t-shirts*

*Anke Steinborn caught this
39.8 lb striped bass 10 miles
from SJM in September 1987*

Satisfied fishermen

On the way to the parade

Mr. Jim Fatt officiating at our wedding ceremony

Prior to the marina being built, Lake Powell reached well up the San Juan River

Taken in 2007, this photograph shows the same view, with Clay Hills Crossing at the bottom, Navajo Mountain top right, Monitor Butte in the center and Paiute Farms center left. The green is mostly tamarisk

had to be re-done costing us additional funds. We wished we had those construction people by the seat of their pants. They must have gotten quite a kickback from all the money that was spent on the initial construction of SJM. We even found out money had been spent to buy equipment that we did not even have at the marina. What? Nothing seemed to surprise us anymore.

DECEMBER 24

The Navajo culture does not embrace the birth of Jesus on December twenty-fifth, but most Navajo celebrate the Anglo spirit of Christmas. They put up Christmas trees and lights and give and receive gifts. Before the employees left for their Christmas holidays, Terry and I planned to have a traditional Anglo Christmas party and exchange gifts with them. We had a name drawing for gifts and everyone was included. A ten-dollar limit was set on the gifts so the exchange would be fun as well as practical. I spent days baking all of my favorite Christmas cookies, candies and breads. We decorated the marina store with a big Christmas tree and many holiday decorations. We invited all of the children of our employees to the celebration, and we provided gifts for them, too. Red shoestrings, colored socks with Native American symbols on them, handmade pottery and old pawn turquoise jewelry were among the many gifts Terry and I received. It seemed that more than one person had drawn our names. It appeared that everyone had a good time and, as always, we hated to see the fun come to an end. It was our first Christmas at SJM and it was special.

DECEMBER 25

Terry and I woke up to a white Christmas. It had snowed again. The sun was shining and the snow glistened like bright diamonds. We felt that all was well within our world at SJM. We were the only humans on the marina property. Everyone else had gone to be with his or her own families for the day. It was the only day that the marina was allowed to be closed to business. One of our gifts from the previous evening had been venison steak. So we had venison for our Christmas dinner. Terry and I sat beside our little skinny but nicely decorated Christmas tree and exchanged gifts. I had hired one the aunts of one of our employees to weave Terry a rug. It was a three by five-foot rectangle and had a gray background with a black and white border. It was especially nice because it had 'a one of a kind' design woven into its center. The design was the logo of SJM. This logo depicted a Navajo man, looking sideways, donning his black cowboy hat and wearing his hair in a bun at the back of his neck secured with white yarn. A *ye''ii* (a Navajo holy figure) encircled the man in red and blue colors. The color of yellow corn stalks represented holy prayers. This logo was unique and it represented everything that was special about our marina and its beginnings. We sat quietly, held hands and gazed fondly and proudly at our new treasure.

DECEMBER 26 – 31

Now what? Well, the bay surrounding the marina had frozen over. For the last few weeks it had been really cold with nighttime temperatures dropping below the zero degree mark. Even the older Navajo could not remember when the bay had frozen like this. Our docks could not stand the strain of the ice against them, and the gas lines on the gas dock might break if the pressure from ice was allowed to build up. The houseboats would not be able to float on top of the ice either. So every afternoon when the temperatures were at their warmest, the houseboats were started up and rammed against the ice to break it up. We did this until there was a path through the ice out onto the river. By keeping the water current under the ice flowing, hopefully the bay would not freeze over. The NPS required that the marina be kept open for business all year round. So that is what we did.

Also during the last few days of the year, a physical year-end inventory had to be taken. This meant that every item at SJM had to be listed and counted. This was another new learning experience for our employees. The keeping account of one's possessions was a foreign concept to the Navajo. Why count and keep track of something? When it was gone, it was gone. But, by now, they were learning that Anglos did some things differently.

It was late into the night when we finished up the inventory. Every single item had been listed and counted. Tomorrow Terry and I would spend New Year's Day adding up and extending the figures so we could get the report to our Albuquerque office by the second of January. Our employees had all gone home or had gone to celebrate the coming of the new year in whatever fashion they chose to. Terry and I were left alone to close the store. We turned off the lights, locked the doors, walked outside and stopped to enjoy the quietness. The night sky was clear and there were thousands of stars visible in the dark midnight-blue canopy above us. They were twinkling brightly and they cast a silvery glow down upon us. The air was cold and we pulled our warm coats up closer to our faces. We hugged each other and gently kissed. Hand in hand we walked toward our home listening to the crunch of the crusted snow under our feet. Before we entered the house, we paused once more, embraced and said, "Happy New Year, San Juan Marina." We hoped it would be.

CHAPTER EIGHT
January 1988
Now the real problems begin

JANUARY 1

Seven months had now come and gone since we first arrived at the marina. Where had the time gone? We had been too busy just trying to keep the marina going to realize what had actually happened as a whole. Now we took time to revel in the many wonderful things that had been achieved. The marina had obtained excellent ratings from the NPS monthly inspections. Houseboats had been rented almost one hundred percent of their season. Customers appeared happy and satisfied and were booking return houseboat trips. Employee attendance was exceptional, and they had completed approximately 80% of their goals in learning how to run and operate a marina. Revenues were very high, and in fact, were higher than had been projected. These were just a few of the successes we experienced. We also realized that through the sharing of our lives at SJM we had gained strength, determination, and unity with our comrades. We were all excited about the approaching year and could envision more success (and revenues) for the marina and ourselves. The confidence of our kids had grown and their energy never waned. It was now time to get prepared for the upcoming season.

JANUARY 2

Because we were in the winter months, our business

had slowed and all of the rental fleet had been taken out of the water. The houseboats sat like great square statues, all in a row, waiting and resting until they would be needed again in the spring. Occasionally a fisherman or two would come and rent a fishing skiff from us, but few customers ventured out onto the cold waters of the San Juan River. The snows came almost daily. The temperatures hovered in the twenty-degree range during the day and plunged below zero during the night. Even the local folks said that they had not seen the weather this cold for at least ten years. The only ones who didn't seem to mind the harsh winter weather conditions were the flocks of geese that landed and swam in the forty-six degree waters of the marina bay. Even our employees could not work outside in such chilly conditions. Refurbishing of the houseboats could not begin until the weather warmed, so we all kept busy by cleaning the store, making out work plans for the refurbishing project and even made lists for repair and replacement parts for the boats. Also, every Saturday morning we held Marina Operation classes in the Store building.

These classes were more of question and answer sessions than organized classes. Someone would bring up a subject that he or she wanted to address and then we would all take part in the discussion. Everything from personal hygiene to accounting procedures was discussed. We reviewed and rewrote the marina operating policies, procedures and job descriptions. Everyone's input was considered. Supply ordering and advertising for the marina were discussed. Role playing was done to learn how to handle customer complaints and problems. Everyone took his or her turn making out employee work schedules. They had all wanted to take the weekends off but soon found out that a marina cannot be run that way. Each employee took his or her turn at being the Manager On Duty for a week at a time. By letting them participate in these activities, and assuming more and more responsibility, they were learning not only how to manage a marina but how to mange themselves as well. They also learned how to interpret the National Park Service's NPS 48 manual and follow all its rules and regulations. Our kids made rapid progress and were becoming more and more self-reliant. This was good.

JANUARY 3 – 5

Having been summoned by our boss Mr. K to the reservations office in Blanding, we arrived to find him talking about his wonderful month-long vacation in Hawaii he had just enjoyed. Mr. K was an older man, in his late sixties, with thinning gray hair and a large round belly. He stood about five feet and eight inches tall and wore chrome-framed glasses. When he smiled, which was not too often, it was clear he had very few teeth. The meeting began and Mr. K informed us there was no money to keep the marina operating. What? He said he was putting a freeze on wages and operating supplies for the marina. The money that had been allotted for houseboat refurbishing and repairs was cancelled. He even wanted to lay off most of the employees, keeping only four along with Terry and myself. Had the man lost his mind? We were also told that it would be at least forty-five days until any money would be considered for marina usage. What was going on?

This was quite an unexpected blow to Terry and me, and it was hard to understand and accept. It was only three months until the season would start again, and we had to have the marina supplied and the houseboats ready to rent. Fifteen houseboats had to be repainted. Repairs to the outsides and insides of the boats had to be made and the motors had to be reconditioned and repaired. Houseboat inventories had to be taken and items replaced. These were normal expenses incurred when renting houseboats. That was no surprise. Renters were always hard on houseboats, but they expected the boats to be shipshape when they rented them. All of these things took time, money, and lots of manpower to get accomplished. We could not wait for forty-five days to start these projects. Why was there no money?

It appeared to Terry and me, from everything we had seen, that SJM had taken in revenues in excess of $750,000 in the seven months since it had opened. The 1988 houseboat rental season looked very promising as well. Most of our customers had taken the $250 refund that they received upon completion of their trip and put it toward another houseboat trip. The reservation office had confirmations and deposits already in their computers for the 1988 season. We were completely booked through June, July, August, and the first half of September. With each customer putting down a $250 deposit, this indicated that approximately $240,000 in advance deposits had been taken in. Now we were being told that there was no money to operate the marina? With our experience in the marina business, we knew something was not right. We were perplexed and angry. Why didn't Mr. K listen to our advice? Why didn't he tell us the truth? (Oh, by the way, he told us, just as the meeting adjourned, that he was taking a month-long trip to China. Sure seemed to us that a lot of money was being spent on his traveling around the world.)

We headed back to the marina with heavy hearts. Well, we are not going to lay off any more employees! Didn't UNI realize that the NPS would have something to say about how the marina was running out of money to operate? Terry and I were not going to let SJM die without a fight. We would find the money somewhere to keep the marina running even if we had to use our own.

JANUARY 6 – 10

There were other issues that remained unsolved at SJM. The treatment plants for purifying water and disposing sewage had not yet been approved. We continued to haul water in and sewage out every day. Two sanitation engineers came to inspect the plants and, we hoped, give approval for their use. However, upon inspection of the lift stations and the sewer pipes, it was discovered that the pipes were initially installed wrong by the marina construction men. (This wasn't the first time that we had discovered that the marina had paid for equipment and services that it did not receive.) By now the continued use of the lift stations was causing elevated stress on the sewer pipes and they might break at any moment. We were instructed to limit our water intake so that our sewage output would lighten the stress on the pipes and the lift stations.

Oops…too late! The pipes broke and now we could not use the lift stations at all. Since we were told, again, that there would be no approval for money to make the needed repairs, we had to order port-a-potties to use. Ridiculous! Also because we now had no way to pump the sewage into the sewage plant, we had to limit our use of water. We were all forced to drive every day into Goulding's Trading Post KOA campground to take showers and do our laundry. This went on for three weeks. We continued to ask for money to get the needed repairs and were constantly told "No." Finally, Terry took matters into his own hands. We spent our own money to buy the needed repair parts and to hire a plumber to fix the pipes and the lift stations. Of course no one was going to reimburse our funds, but we felt it was important to keep the marina running. We were asked to make a complete report to the NPS after they found out during one of their monthly inspections what had been happening. The marina concession contract would have been in jeopardy if the repairs had not been made. Evidently, UNI and Mr. K did not care, but we did. So the marina was saved again, and we were all glad when our sewer trauma was over. And, on the lighter side: our port-a-potties were delivered and pumped out by a company named The Honey Pots that was owned by a man named Mr. Flowers. Honestly, it was the truth!

JANUARY 11

What could possibly happen next? It wasn't long before we knew. A gas leak had been reported at the gasoline pumps down on the docks. Gas was rapidly dripping into the water. This was indeed an emergency and, whether we had money approved to make repairs or not, we had to have the pumps fixed. We called the company that supplied our gas pumps and they came quickly and fixed the leak. Meanwhile, we put the proper environmental products into the water to contain the gasoline. When the repairs were completed, we heaved a sigh of relief that was only short-lived. While talking with the gas company repairmen, we learned that the original contract between SJM and UNI had never been signed. The gas company had not been paid for the rental of the equipment or for any of the gas it had delivered all year long. It was only out of the generosity of their hearts that they had made the requested repairs for us. We did not know what to say. They knew that Terry and I were not to blame as we were only the marina managers. What was going on with Mr. K and UNI? It seemed with each new emergency, we were accidentally discovering more and more facts about our employers that made us think that the monster of fraud was beginning to raise its ugly head. Something was definitely wrong.

JANUARY 12 – 14

In the midst of seeing that the daily operation of the marina continued, doing repairs, and keeping the equipment maintained, Terry and I were involved in finding a permanent site for SJM. The future of the marina had always been overshadowed with the problem of finding a permanent home for it. We knew from its conception that the site where the marina was located was only a temporary spot and that this location had about a five-year life expectancy. The contract between the NPS and the Navajo Nation called for a permanent site to be chosen, and a new marina built before the temporary site at Paiute Farms would be abandoned. That is why we were hired to train the Navajo to be able to manage the new marina when it was ready. We were ready, but the permanent site had not even been chosen yet.

Due to the expected build up and eventual silting in of the bay where we were now located, the present site of SJM was unacceptable. The San Juan River was a fast moving river and the silt it carried with it accumulated into our bay. NPS studies had shown that the silt build up was progressing much faster that originally expected. Now it looked like the five-year prediction was not correct. San Juan Marina would have only one to two years before our bay would be silted over. A permanent site must be chosen quickly. There were two possible canyons being considered for the next marina site. One was down river about ten miles at Copper Canyon, and the other was an additional fifteen miles further down river, at Neskhai Canyon. Each had large, deep bays that would accommodate the proposed houseboat rental expansion. But there were many major issues that needed to be addressed before either of these canyons could be approved. First of all, there were no existing roads to either of these canyons. Since most of the land south of the San Juan River was Navajo Reservation, and since most of this land had grazing rights held by the local Navajo families, it would be very difficult to obtain permits to cross their land. Secondly, many bridges would have to be built to accommodate the new roads into the canyons. All of these things cost time and lots of money. But time was running out, and no one wanted to commit the money for such a project. At several meetings, many of which Terry and I attended, the NPS reminded the Navajo Nation that the move to the permanent site had to be made soon if it wanted to fulfill its contract. If it didn't, the marina would have to close. SJM could not remain at Paiute Farms.

So our next project included a trip over the tall mesa that stood between the area where we were located and Copper Canyon. Monitor Butte was over six thousand feet high and had neither trail nor road to follow to get to its top. Our scouts were to go up to the top and try to find a path or trail that could be turned into a road that could be built to Copper Canyon. Terry and Bart, Jerry Sampson (a well known marina consultant and our friend), Dick Natosie (a UNI representative) and Fred Ladman (an engineer with Plateau Resources who had done the original plans for SJM) were going to be hiking the entire day across the mesa. I was to meet them that evening at Copper Canyon with one of our houseboats.

The guys had to pick their way gingerly to the top of the mesa, winding back and forth, making their own trail as they went. The soft shale and loose gravel among the sandstone rocks and boulders made their climb long and tiresome. They had to pick and choose their footing carefully. It took them about three hours to reach the top where they paused to catch breath. They were high enough that nothing could spoil their magnificent view. They could see in all directions for over a hundred miles: the Blue Mountains in the north, Sleeping Ute Mountain to the east, the sacred Navajo Mountain to the south, and the Henry Mountains to the west. The crystal clear blue sky made everything appear close enough to touch. In the distance they could see local Navajo attending their herds of sheep and goats. It looked like an animated painting. It took one's breath away.

On top of the mesa there were small patches of short, dark green scrub trees mixed among the taller blue green pinyon pines to walk through. Every now and then remains of an ancient Anasazi Kiva could be found. The Anasazi (or the Ancestral Puebloans as they are also called) were the people that had lived on top of the mesas 1400 years ago and had mysteriously disappeared long before the Navajo had come into this part of the country. Among the ruins, the hikers found arrowhead chipping grounds and the remains of storage granaries. This place gave everyone the surreal feeling of being on sacred ground. So as they explored, they were careful not to disturb anything, and they spoke softly so as not to upset any Anasazi spirits that may have been left to guard their old homes.

Traveling across the top of the mesa was much easier than the climb up. After a short rest and a drink of water from their canteens, they continued on. The top of the mesa was about three miles across and fairly flat. Birds were plentiful as were small, inquisitive kangaroo rats and playful ground squirrels. There were tracks of coyotes and bobcats. It had been rumored that there could be wild horses on Monitor Butte but none were seen on this trip.

As they hiked along the men spoke of many things. They talked about how Terry had worked for Jerry for several years, and how Jerry had taught him the marina business and of the many good times they had shared. Jerry told stories of how he had explored the Lake Powell area and of the many things he had discovered. Bart told of how he had herded sheep and goats in the area, and of how he had ridden his horses on the mesa and the strange and wonderful things he had seen. Fred told of his own visits to this area and what things he had experienced about this wonderful land and the people who lived here.

Midday approached and the men stopped for lunch. The early morning air had been cool, but now the warm January noonday sum warmed everyone's shoulders. After a quick sack lunch of dried beef jerky and oranges and more water, the hike continued. It would be several more hours before they would enjoy a hot meal and a good rest aboard a houseboat.

As the hikers had started out that morning, I was getting ready to board a houseboat at the marina. The supplies of food and blankets had been gathered up the night before and I was ready to start my way to Copper Canyon on the water. The bay had frozen around the houseboats again during the night so I had to figure some way of getting the houseboat through the ice and out into the clear unfrozen river channel. Slowly I put the engines into reverse and gave them power. Crunch, crunch went the ice. Stopping, I put the engines into the forward position and gave them more power. Ccrraaaaakkkk! The ice broke in front of me. Back and forth I powered the houseboat until I had made a big enough hole to turn the boat around. I headed toward the fast moving water of the San Juan River and Lake Powell. It was good that I had lots of faith in the sturdiness of the pontoons on that boat. Finally, after about two hours of maneuvering back and forth and inching my way forward, I had the houseboat in deep running water and was headed toward Copper Canyon.

There were ten miles to go before I would reach my destination. On the way I saw a coyote with her two small pups drinking at the river's edge. Mother coyote looked up but seemed to know that I presented no threat to her or her family and went back to drinking. There were several ravens squawking above the houseboat as if they were giving me directions. When they were silent, I could hear the wind swoosh through their wings as they flew by. I even had the rare opportunity to see a golden eagle. Watching that magnificent bird gave me a peaceful and hopeful feeling as I viewed their presence as an omen of good luck. Driving on down the river I thought of the guys hiking the mesa. It would be fun to hear how their day had gone and what they had discovered. Approaching the entrance to Copper Canyon, I slowed the houseboat. Finding a shallow sandy spot on a nearby beach, I eased the houseboat forward for a gentle landing. I was very proud of my ability to maneuver the boat and wished that someone (especially the men) had been watching to cheer at my success. I put down the anchors and tied the boat safely to shore. I put on the coffee, prepared and warmed the chili and hot bread that I had brought and lit the propane heaters on the houseboat for warmth. The sun was setting and twilight was falling. Soon the sky would be dark, and blackness would settle around the houseboat. The night air started to feel very cool. Patiently I waited for the hikers.

Starting down the other side of the Mesa was not much easier than the climb up had been. Several times the hikers had to turn back and find better footing as the ground slid under their boots. If a road could be built into Copper Canyon this was the way in which it would have to be done: traverse the canyon walls and build several bridges to go over the ravines. That would be very, very expensive. Also there were the grazing leases of the local Navajo who lived in Copper Canyon to deal with. These folks would not be anxious to have their grazing land dug up for roads that would bring outsiders into their world. It seemed like there would be too many obstacles to overcome.

As the hikers reached the bottom of the mesa and joined Copper Canyon, their walk to the houseboat went fast. The darkness had enveloped them. Looking ahead they began to see the yellow hue of the lights inside the awaiting boat. They were tired, cold and hungry. We sat around the cabin table and ate our hot meal and reviewed the day's events. It wasn't long until we retired into warm sleeping bags and fell quickly to sleep. It had been another good day in Navajoland.

The next morning the sun was already high in the sky by the time we were all up, fed and starting down river to check out Neskhai Canyon, the second possible permanent site for SJM. Its bay was large and deep. It was also protected from the prevailing west and north winds by high cliffs. There was enough flat land adjacent to the bay that proposed buildings such as a hotel, a restaurant or two, or even casinos could be built. But the building of a road into Neskhai Canyon would be even more of a challenge that a road into Copper Canyon. Well, all we could do was report what we saw and give the NPS and the Navajo Nation our best recommendations. We turned the houseboat homeward toward SJM and agreed that a decision would have to be forthcoming if the marina was to survive. What would be the outcome we wondered?

JANUARY 18
Today we spent all day at an Oljato Chapter House meeting. Now I know why our employees fondly referred it to as a "chatter house." Everyone attending sometimes all talked at once. All of our employees and their families attended the meeting to show their support for the marina. Two of the local elders of the Oljato community who supported SJM were Mr. Jim Fatt and Mr. Walter Ateen. These two well respected leaders of the community were representative of traditional Navajo thinking. Their very presence seemed to invoke pride and perseverance of the Navajo spirit. When they spoke, everyone grew silent and respectfully listened until they finished. After hearing the English translation of their speeches, it was apparent that dissension had fallen between two Navajo political groups in their support of the marina. Many questions had been raised as to why employees had been laid off. Our employer, UNI, had told these people that the purpose of SJM was to provide economic development and increased revenues to their chapter. Why were their children not working, and where were all the increased revenues that they had been promised? As the discussions continued, the mood of the people kept getting more and more terse. The men who came to represent our employer were not able to answer the questions to our Olajto friends' satisfaction. As we sat and listened, it became apparent that bad debts, repayment of old loans and plain old job greasing by our employer had put SJM in the middle of a political upheaval that Terry and I would not have any control over. All we cared about was keeping the kids working and the marina running and making our customers happy. We wondered if we

would ever know the whole story.

Modern Anglo business concepts were foreign to the uncomplicated way the traditional Navajo thought things through. They saw the result of good business management and the dollars that the Anglos had in their pockets and how they lived, but they didn't clearly see the formulas and procedures required to get to that point. Too, we think the language differences caused misinterpretations of meanings of many of the business concepts and planned goals. They did know, however, that Terry and I were on their side. They trusted us and believed in our efforts to help their children. They deserved and wanted honest answers. However, on this day, that was not going to be accomplished, because the representatives of our employer kept sidestepping the questions. Eventually everyone got so frustrated that they just went home. Let the politics go to the Devil.

JANUARY 19 – 24

We had decided to ignore the freeze on expenditures that Mr. K had put on us in the beginning of January. We would invest our own money to keep the marina going. We felt it was important to help the employees proceed with the plans to produce new brochures for the upcoming year. For weeks everyone took pictures of our marina and the houseboats. The scenery on the San Juan River is breathtaking and we hoped to capture it in our brochures. The boat rental rates were increased by a small percent after we got permission from the NPS. Four major advertising opportunities, boat shows, were quickly approaching, so we needed the new brochures soon. The upcoming boat shows, one in Phoenix, Arizona, one in Denver, Colorado, another in Pomona, California, and the last in Albuquerque, New Mexico, were the most attended boat shows in the Southwest. Attending a boat show, passing out brochures, and talking directly with potential customers was the best way to increase revenues with the least amount of money spent for advertising. It had been claimed that we could reach an estimated 500,000 potential customers. Now that is a lot of people, and that meant a lot of potential business revenues for San Juan Marina.

JANUARY 25 – 26

There were always many rumors floating around SJM. Now ugly rumors of deceit and double-dealings about the upper management of our parent company, UNI, were filtering down to us. It was rumored that everyone, including the Navajo chairman, was involved in shady exchanges of monies that were supposed to go for the economic development of the local Navajo chapter and its people. The local Navajo people were beginning to direct more and more of their questions to their government officials at Window Rock, the capital of the Navajo Nation. Finally two of the top Navajo government representatives showed up at SJM. They questioned us and our employees about what was going on at the marina. We answered all of their questions as honestly as we could. They said they could see the potential financial success that the marina should be able to provide to the local community. They also realized that the rumored problems did not originate at SJM but with the management of the company, UNI, that had the contract with the NPS. The Navajo chairman had already put the political agenda of the Navajo Nation in jeopardy, and these two men had been appointed to sort out the rising intergovernmental problems at Window Rock. SJM was just a small branch on a much larger, apparently much abused tree and solving the marina problems was not at the top of their agenda. We knew we were not the problem, but unfortunately we did not have the solutions to the problems. All that we could do now, was to carry on the best we knew how.

Another chapter meeting had been called and Terry had been asked to speak. This meeting would be held at the Navajo Mountain Chapter House on Navajo Mountain, one of the four sacred mountains that form the boundary of Navajoland. We rode with Pamela, our Navajo NPS Liaison, to the Chapter meeting. She would provide the English interpretation for us. She drove her four-wheel Jeep, as the roads we would travel over would require such a vehicle. It was early afternoon when we left the marina and headed west. Pamela was taking us to an area not easily accessible by car and known only to local Navajo. After leaving the paved road, we turned onto a dirt road. Continuing on, we followed an old Navajo trail across the top of a long ridge. The sun was setting as we stopped on top of the ridge to take in the spectacular view in front of us. Canyons on either side of us fell into deep abysses covered by red sandstone rocks and juniper trees. We could not see to the bottom. The low setting sun caused the cliffs to turn from red to deep purple. Other mountain ranges and foothills stretched out before us, and we felt so small. Looking out we could see across Navajo land for hundreds of miles. It seemed as if we magically floated above it all. No wonder the Navajo didn't signpost this trail.

The sunset came and went as we traveled on toward our destination. The warm glow of lights inside the chapter house greeted us at the end of a dark dirt road. Many Navajo were inside talking as the meeting had already started. After being greeted warmly with smiles and handshakes in proper Navajo fashion, we took our seats. We sat quietly and gave our attention to each speaker as the meeting continued. Finally, it was Terry's turn to speak. He spoke about the San Juan Marina, its employees, and its intended purpose. He and Pamela answered a few questions, and Terry invited everyone to come to the marina and see how things were being done. They all seemed to appreciate that we had given them a special invitation.

After Terry spoke, a special award was presented to one of the Navajo men who had been a Code Talker in World War II. We had never heard of the Code Talkers so this was very interesting to us. In WWII the Allies had codes that the Japanese eventually began to break and decode, making our communications ineffective. Then, in 1941, an idea surfaced among our leaders to develop a new code using Navajo words for English words and letters. Only Navajo men could do the code talking because it had to be done by memory and Navajo is a hard language to learn to speak. At first Washington only used the Code Talkers as runners to deliver messages. But as their success increased, and it became apparent that the Japanese could not break the new code, the Code Talkers were used more and more. They became as useful as any weapon the military had, and these men had personal protection wherever they went. Without the Navajo Code Talkers, World War II would have been much harder to win. Out of approximately 3600 Navajo in WWII, 400 were Code Talkers. Sadly, they received no recognition for their efforts until 1970, when the Navajo Code Talkers Association was founded. Then the Code Talkers and the important part they played in our history were made public. Recently a movie entitled "Wind Talkers" was made to show what the Navajo Code Talkers went through and did for our nation. Be sure to watch it.

JANUARY 31

Today we had a very special arrival at SJM! Our employee, Mary Ann, and her husband Abe, welcomed their first child, a son, into the world. Mary Ann was our accountant/administration assistant. Her pregnancy had made her a little plump but she still had a very attractive figure. She was a beautiful young woman whose soft, gentle smile could melt your heart. Her husband, Abe, was a dockhand and helped with other duties. He was tall and thin and he wore round, gold-rimmed glasses. He wore his hair short in a flat top style. We could always count on Abe and Mary Ann to do whatever was asked and to help wherever they were needed.

Sometimes in the Navajo tradition, a name was not given as soon as a baby is born. The parents might wait to see "what name the baby chose" or wait for a sign to determine the baby's name. But Mary Ann and Abe had chosen the name of their son, Justin, and it seemed to fit him well. Mary Ann delivered her son at the local hospital and included many of the private Navajo traditions that accompany a birth, in her labor and delivery. Justin weighed nine pounds two ounces and was twenty-one inches long. With plenty of long black hair and chubby little brown cheeks he made his parents smile with pride. In fact, we were all proud! He was immediately put into a traditional Navajo cradleboard. Traditionally, most infants remained in the cradleboard, being taken out only for feeding and changing, until the age of one or longer. The cradleboard design made carrying the baby much easier for the mother and gave the baby a feeling of security. With the extended family members of Justin's family, he would not want for babysitters. I hoped to be included in the babysitting list, too.

CHAPTER NINE
February 1988
Boat Shows

FEBRUARY 1 – 7

During the first week of February, days were quiet at SJM. Daylight hours were short and the weather unpredictable. Temperatures were cold and the canyon winds were continuous and sometimes fierce. At times like these it was easier to sit and drink hot coffee than brave the outside elements. Since we had laid off half of our employees, there were few of us left to do the work. We kept busy cleaning the store, the offices and the inside of the houseboats. If the weather permitted, the employees worked on the outside of the houseboats, repairing and refurbishing them. The pontoons on each houseboat still had to be sandblasted to remove the algae buildup and the rust that had accumulated on them during the summer months. After that, the pontoons would be repainted with a very thick tar-like paint that protected them from the next season's use. The weather had to be at least seventy degrees before the paint would adhere properly to the pontoons, so we would have to wait for warmer days to start the pontoon project.

There were rumors of more employee layoffs, wages being cut in half and possible cancellations of approved advertising opportunities and boat shows. When we went to another meeting with Mr. K, we found out that some of the rumors were true. He had demoted and cut the wages of Rita, the reservation office manager, and he fired the head accountant. (Probably because he knew too many damaging facts against him. The head accountant reported that Mr. K had a plan to bankrupt UNI and take all of the funds from SJM for himself. The office manager knew that the files on the computers had been tampered with, and she had retrieved back up files to prove it. The accounts and the monies were all going to be moved to Mr. K's personal business office in Albuquerque. All vendors would now correspond with the office there and the marina was now on a COD basis for the vendors. (The fired accountant said that, in reality, it was the vendors who were putting SJM on the COD restrictions because most of them had not been paid since the marina had opened in May of 1987.) Mr. K also cancelled one of the prepaid travel/boat shows that we had planned to attend. Only one houseboat booking from that show would have paid for the show fees, our travel expenses and our wages. Why did the boss ask our opinion about things if he wasn't going to listen to us? We had the experience needed to promote the marina, and we knew that by not going to this travel show we had lost a good economical chance for SJM. Well, there was one last order given to us by Mr. K. Terry and I were to redo the approved budget for the year and have a new one ready to present to him in three days. (By the way, we were also instructed to give free houseboat trips to those whom our boss would choose. We suspected that those trips were "trade outs" for goods and services for our boss, but we would not be able to prove it.) Terry and I headed back to the marina with heavy hearts and got to work preparing a new budget.

FEBRUARY 8 – 14

On the designated day, we flew to Albuquerque to meet with Mr. K. After a brief tour of his personal business, a clothing plant, we gathered in his office for our meeting. We sat in silence as Mr. K reviewed the new budget. He looked up after reviewing the budget and told us that it was not satisfactory. He continued on by telling us that there was absolutely no money available for refurbishing the boats or for supplies. We were told that we had to "make do with what we had." Terry and I sat in silence. We did not understand. Why was there no money? A long discussion followed and we pressed the boss for believable answers.

After questioning our boss for about an hour concerning the whereabouts of funds that we knew had been collected by SJM and sent to the main office, we were told something that we found hard to believe. He told us that all profits from SJM, for the next fifteen years, were going to go to another Navajo company to pay back loans that our parent company, UNI, had borrowed. The amount that was to be paid back exceeded $4,000,000. The money would not be put back into SJM. As far as we could tell, the aforementioned loans had nothing to do with SJM. What were Mr. K and UNI really involved in? Well, the NPS would not look upon this information favorably. Terry remained calm, but my temper grew, and I knew I would say something I shouldn't if I stayed. I excused myself to go the rest room and said I would be right back. But I had no intention of returning to that room. Instead I took a long walk around the building to regain my composure and was still walking when Terry came and found me. "We have to finish this meeting up, and then you and I will do what we have to do. We have to get some help with this situation," he said.

Now, in retrospect, I suppose neither the NPS nor the Navajo Nation really cared what our parent company did with its profits as long as SJM was kept running, customers were happy and the NPS contract requirements were being fulfilled. After all, the NPS had forfeited the normal five percent of the gross fee charge to the Navajo Nation to help their economic development program. However, we were sure the NPS thought it prudent to reinvest the monies made at SJM back into the marina so there would be enough money for the relocation and proposed expanded development of the permanent site. Wait until they heard what was happening! We began to realize that we were up against real problems, most of which were beyond our control. We knew that the marina and the employees were in jeopardy, and that we would have to be very careful how we handled things from now on.

The purpose of the original marina contract between the NPS and the Navajo Nation had been to promote economic development and jobs for the Navajo people, especially those Navajo who lived on the northern part of the reservation known as the Utah Strip. This was where SJM was located. However, none of the local Navajo were receiving any monies from the profits of SJM. They began to ask questions. Also, the NPS began getting phone calls from unpaid vendors. These vendors had not received any payments, and they were not getting answers or cooperation from our home office in Albuquerque as to why they had not been paid. They repeatedly received the answer that their check was in the mail.

The NPS required an annual financial report from UNI. If this report was not filed or received on time, SJM would receive an unsatisfactory rating. Three unsatisfactory ratings acquired within one year would result in a violation of the contract and the marina would be closed and the contract terminated. Well we were just informed by the NPS that the marina had received its first unsatisfactory rating! Terry and I had always kept our employees informed of all events concerning the marina, good and bad. After all, they had to learn everything it took to work, operate and manage a marina and to do so within the NPS guidelines and contract obligations. Now we had to tell them about the unsatisfactory rating. This information hit all of us at the marina very hard. We had been proud of our continual excellent ratings on all of our inspections at the marina. The fault did not lie with us. Apparently UNI had not submitted the required financial report and had told the NPS that they had no intention of doing so in the near future. What were they thinking? The employees could see the potential of SJM as well as the consequences if our parent company failed to cooperate with the NPS. Well, we couldn't worry about it now. We had two boat/travel shows to attend and we had to get on with the running of a marina. We would let the NPS fight it out with UNI and Mr. K.

FEBRUARY 15 – 20

One of the most valuable, and perhaps the most important, advertising tools for the marina business is having a booth at a boat/travel show. There were twenty-three of these shows held every year at every major city in the Southwest at the time. The potential of getting business for a marina from one of these shows was staggering and the expenses involved were minimal. These Boat/Travel shows were prescheduled events held in large civic centers or at fairground buildings so that large crowds could attend. Boat companies, sport and recreation vehicle companies and travel and resort companies all paid for booths so they could advertise their products. Some booths were large, showing big boats, RVs and sports equipment and supplies. Other booths were small and held tables with brochures on them. Everyone wanted to get their brochures in the hands of every potential customer. These shows were the best and most efficient way to advertise to the most people at one time.

The first boat/travel show for San Juan Marina was held in Phoenix, Arizona. Terry and I took Sandy with us to do the show since she was our houseboat reservations manager. Sandy was not shy, could speak fluent English and was knowledgeable about houseboat rentals. She would be able to represent the Navajo people well and answer all questions that might be asked. Many of the tourists had heard of the new SJM through the newspapers and by word of mouth at Lake Powell.

Many more had not heard of it and were excited that more of Lake Powell would be open to exploration because of the supplies, namely the availability of gasoline, at SJM.

Now, to the average onlooker, presiding over a booth at a boat/travel show looked like a lot of fun, and it was. But it was a lot of hard work, too. The hours were long and your feet and legs became really tired. You talked until your voice was scratchy, and your face hurt from smiling. There were never bathroom or eating breaks because you didn't want to miss the chance of selling your product. But the rewards came when you saw the smiles and the excitement the customers showed and the possibility of a potential booking.

Over the next four days we met approximately 30,000 people. We passed out our brochures to each and every person that stopped by our booth, and we answered question upon question. We wore our Navajo clothes and turquoise jewelry and looked quite handsome. On the curtain backdrop behind our table we hung large 16" x 20" photographs of Lake Powell and the Monument Valley area. We greeted everyone with the Navajo hello and enjoyed all of the new attention that SJM and we generated. We took four confirmed houseboat reservations during the show, and the phones were ringing off the hook at our reservations office back at the marina. We felt we were off to a good start for the coming season. However, our nagging problems only left our minds for a short while. On our way home to SJM, we stopped at our boat motor distributor. We were going to pick up some repair parts to take back with us. Again, we found out that this vendor had never been paid and that we were on a COD basis with him. In fact, he threatened to repossess our motors. We couldn't blame him and asked him to address the NPS with his concerns, not just our boss. We were getting more and more uncomfortable with these situations that were not under our control.

The weather had warmed up enough to sandblast the pontoons on the fifteen houseboats that we rented. All of the houseboats had been pulled out of the water and were blocked high into the air. Each boat was perched upon four pillars of sturdy wooden blocks. By blocking the houseboats high into the air the employees could have easy access to the pontoons. Because of our money restrictions we were not able to buy the sand that we needed to use in the sandblasting machine we had rented. So our employees had the idea of getting the sand out of the river. But the river sand was too coarse for the sandblasting machine. It had to be shaken and sifted through screens until we got the finest grade of sand we could get. Some of the employees dug up the sand at the edge of the river and loaded it into the back of pickup trucks. Other employees unloaded the sand into piles by the sandblasting machine. We all took turns sifting the sand over and over, through screen after screen, again and again until we got what we needed. It took a lot of sand.

The sandblasting machine had a hose with a porcelain tip on it. The sand was forced through the hose and out through the tip by compressed air. Each porcelain tip was fragile and cost forty dollars per tip to replace. Since the tips underwent great stress they broke easily. We had no money to replace broken porcelain tips either. So our employees again put their heads together and came up with a great solution. They gathered old spark plugs and retrofitted them to the hose on the sandblasting machine. It worked! We finished sandblasting all of the pontoons on the houseboats within one week. It is true that "Necessity is the mother of invention."

The pontoons on the houseboats could now be painted. Bitoxy is a special, high cost, asphalt-based coating that protects the pontoons from corrosion and algae build up. This type of coating is very thick, like the consistency of tar. It is put on with paint rollers instead of brushes. All equipment used and all clothes worn that come in contact with the Bitoxy have to be thrown away. It is nasty stuff, and you do not want to get it on your skin or in your hair. So, covered from head to toe in our raggedy clothes, gloves and headscarves, we proceeded to paint the pontoons. It took almost three weeks to finish. But finish it we did. Whew!

FEBRUARY 24 – 29

It was now time to attend our second boat/travel show. We took Rita from the home office with us this time. She had been the Rental Reservations Manager and had never been to a boat/travel show. After her wages were reduced and the accounts were moved to Albuquerque, Rita informed Mr. K that she was going to go to the Navajo chairman at Window Rock and spill the beans about what was happening with UNI and Mr. K. He threatened to prosecute her if she did, so Rita was ready to fight back any way she could. She wanted to see SJM and her people succeed. So she volunteered to help us with the boat show. She was excited and looked forward to a fun and educational trip. After our long ride to Denver we settled into our hotel. The next morning we arrived early at the Denver Coliseum and found our booth quickly. We set up our table, hung our pictures and stacked up our brochures. It was a very, very busy week. We talked to approximately 75,000 people! We answered questions, passed out thousands of brochures and took many reservations and bookings for the up-coming season. If all of the people came to SJM that said they would, we would have more business than we could handle.

The success of our trip to Denver was shortlived; we arrived home to sad news. Our NPS Ranger, Gary, had decided to leave SJM. It was true that he was getting a promotion, which he richly deserved, and we were happy for him but, oh, how we would miss him. Godspeed, friend, we wish you well. We will never forget you.

CHAPTER TEN
March 1988
Fixing Houseboats

MARCH 1 – 4

Terry and I spent most of our time trying to keep the employees motivated and to keep the marina running amid all of our financial problems. Our marina season would be in full swing within two months, and at the rate we were going, we feared we would not be ready. The vendors had not yet been paid, and communication had broken down between our boss and us. Thankfully, the NPS remained our ally. They continued to have faith in us and confidence in our abilities to run the marina but our stress level was still way too high.

We were all trying hard to make the marina a success, but we could not keep the marina running without money to buy supplies and product to sell. We wondered if the officials of the Navajo Nation actually understood the magnitude of the problems we were having and the marina's potential. Maybe if they had known, they would have intervened and taken the authority away from UNI and Mr. K. The local Navajo people, and especially our employees, should have been in charge of their own destiny. After all, this was the original intent of the marina contract. Maybe the Navajo Nation leaders did not know what was happening. Each and every time Terry and I had met with the tribal representatives, they praised our efforts and seemed pleased with the progress at SJM. Terry and I were scheduled for another meeting with Mr. K but we chose to ignore it. We were sure this would really anger him, however, we really didn't care. We were now declaring war! If we had really thought he would have listened to us and changed his attitude and actions toward SJM and its employees, we would have tried harder to communicate with him but, thus far, he had given us no sign that he understood how a marina should be run. He still insisted that there was no money for operating SJM. This just couldn't be. We knew that there had been profits. Now we also knew that most of those profits had gone for other companies and not been put aside for SJM. The boss had admitted it. We didn't believe that this was the way the NPS intended for SJM to be run. We wouldn't let SJM go down without a fight.

MARCH 5 – 9

We had a meeting with representatives from the NPS and the Navajo Nation. They asked us to tell them how SJM was doing and if we had any problems. So we told them. We revealed the problems regarding the restrictions put upon us. We told them that the vendors had been asking for their bills to be paid before they would service us. We told them and showed them the written proof that UNI and Mr. K were in twelve violations of the NPS contract. Now UNI had already received one marginal score for their failure to comply with NPS. The NPS representatives knew that Terry and I had done everything within our power and authority for SJM and its employees. We had complied with all NPS regulations and had received excellent ratings. The NPS and the Navajo Nation representatives listened, and we saw that they could not believe what they were hearing. But they did know we were telling the truth. Mr. K was also scheduled to have been at this meeting but failed to show. Later when he was confronted, our boss said that all the payments for the overdue bills "have been paid." What a fibber.

MARCH 10 – 12

While working at other marinas we had learned that souvenirs and most tee shirts were ordered during the winter months and were scheduled for spring delivery. We knew we could get dated payments with most of the vendors we would be ordering from. Dated payment was a payment plan where the marina did not have to pay the vendor for the souvenirs or tee shirts until they were delivered. Not only could we pay upon delivery but also we negotiated for a partial payment plan in three installments. We would also receive additional discounts for the quantities we ordered. It was the way that most souvenir vendors operated. After all, it took time to compile the orders, design the logos and then get the tee shirts printed and delivered. By the time the first shipment would be sold there would be enough money to pay for the second shipment.

After meeting with several souvenir vendors we filled out the appropriate purchase order requests and sent them to Mr. K for approval. He approved them and sent them back to us so we could place our orders. But then, the very next day, he cancelled the purchase orders requests. Next he sent us tee shirts from the clothing company he personally owned. When the tee shirts arrived we found scorched marks on them, crooked logos, unsewn seams, and the quality in general was poor. What a disgrace! We packed up all of the tee shirts and sent them right back to him. Terry and I implemented our own plan to purchase the souvenirs and tee shirts we needed. As the tee shirts and souvenirs sold, we saved back the money and paid the vendors ourselves. We felt this was the only option we had.

MARCH 13 – 18

Every day became more upsetting than the last. We tested the houseboats' water systems and found that many of the water pipes had leaks in them. The water pipes apparently broke during the very cold winter months. Several pipes had to be replaced before we could put the boats back into the water and begin renting them. There was, apparently, still no money approved for these repairs. So again, Terry and I scraped up enough money from our pockets to get the supplies to make the repairs. After the repairs were made the houseboats were put back into the water. Now the motors that powered the houseboats were tested. Yes, there were motor repairs that needed to be made, too. Fortunately, the repairs on the houseboat motors were minimal, and we had enough spare parts and good mechanics to get the repairs made smoothly and quickly, and we didn't have to dig into our own pockets for the money. The maids cleaned and restocked the houseboats during the rest of the month, and we were ready for our upcoming rental season. We all heaved a small sigh of relief.

MARCH 19 – 30

As previously discussed, the NPS had not wanted to open SJM without the water and sewer systems in place and in working order. But they knew the Navajo Nation needed the marina to be open so that they could begin to take in revenues. So the NPS made an exception and let SJM open with one specific condition: the water and sewer system had to be approved as soon as possible. We had now been open for business for ten months and still we had no approved water/sewer system. Mr. K never said why he had not made getting the water/sewage situation a priority, but we figured that he was relying on the generous and patient nature of the NPS to overlook his neglect. Water samples were being sent daily to the required agencies. We kept the water plant running every day, putting in the required chemicals. However, it wasn't long before we ran out of the chemicals needed to keep the water plant running. The chemicals were very expensive and, of course, Mr. K was refusing to spend the money to buy them. As a result, we were not able to keep the water plant running and the testing stopped.

This was not a good situation.

The hauling of water and sewage was also very expensive and required many man-hours of labor. Because of the rough terrain, the equipment often broke down. There were always flat tires to fix, diesel fuel to be bought and many other numerous repairs to be made to the tractor truck and hauling containers. Now, Big Blue, as we fondly called the truck, had broken down again. The clutch went out, and we were unable to haul water or sewage. For two days we tried to get permission from Mr. K to get money to fix the truck but to no avail. We were getting thirsty and constipated. We finally got approval, but it was not to fix the truck. Mr. K told us to hire a truck and a driver from Blanding, a town ninety miles one way from SJM, to haul our water and sewage every day. We didn't know how long the truck would remain broken down, but wouldn't it have been less expensive to fix it than hire the hauling done by someone else? (Of course, Mr. K probably had no intention of paying the truck driver.)

MARCH 31

We had another NPS inspection, and we passed with an excellent score. We had gotten excellent scores on all of our inspections since the marina had been opened and we were proud. But the scores at the marina made up only one-half of the final total score. Not only had UNI received one marginal rating for failure to submit their annual financial report, now they were receiving another marginal rating. The reason for the second marginal rating was due to the failure of UNI and Mr. K to see that the water and the sewer plants had been approved and properly implemented for the safety of the employees and customers of SJM. The contract between the Navajo Nation and the NPS was now in jeopardy. The NPS warned they would close down SJM on June 1st if the water/sewer systems were not approved and operational. As bad as it seemed, this provided a ray of light and hope that SJM might draw enough attention to keep it running and get a more suitable and caring management.

CHAPTER ELEVEN
April 1988
Trouble Ahead

APRIL 1 – 3

It was Easter Sunday and everything was quiet as I stepped out the back door of our mobile home. I had gotten up early, as I often did, taken my hot cup of coffee and sat down on the nearby wooden steps. I rested my elbows on my knees and held my cup with both hands close to my face. The warm wonderful smell of fresh rich coffee filled my nostrils. From the elevated position of our mobile home, I could gaze out and see the whole marina compound and the lake. The blue-violet sky in the east quickly turned pink, as the sun started to rise. During the next few minutes the sky became orange and then yellow and then blue as the sun made his journey to the west. There were no clouds in the sky, not even on the horizon. It would be a warm clear day. The water around the marina appeared as smooth as glass, and it reflected the dark red mesas that rose up around it. It was a peaceful and beautiful sight. I loved this time of the day. Soon employees and customers would be bustling around the marina, and my few quiet moments would be gone. I would then again be involved with the many tasks of running this marina.

I sighed long and slow as I sat and reflected on the last ten months. What was going to happen to this little marina and its employees? Why didn't everyone see the beauty of this area and its people and the potential of the marina like we did? We had so much to be thankful for this Easter day. It had been our destiny to be involved with SJM and we would always be glad to have had this experience. I looked into the sky above and listened to the whoosh of the air through the wings of a raven that flew overhead. A soft warm breeze gently caressed me, and I suddenly knew that no matter what happened in the days ahead, our lives would never be the same. We would always be connected to the people here. Our hearts and souls were now part of this land and the *Diné*.

Easter weekend always marked the start of the summer rental season for any marina. The same was true for us. We were renting eleven houseboats this weekend, and our customer visitation was good. We were glad to see the return of business from our customers and hear their enthusiasm for SJM's continued success. The weather, traditionally always cool and windy at Easter time, was unseasonably warm, sunny and calm. All the women employees wore Easter bonnets of all types, and we adorned them with colorful assorted silk flowers and many diverse colored ribbons. This made our customers smile, and they appreciated our humor. We passed out jellybeans and chocolate egg candy. Everyone seemed to enjoy the special way we made his or her visit personal and fun.

APRIL 4 – 10

As we awoke this morning, we wondered why it felt so cold in our home. Upon investigation, Terry found out that we had no heat, no lights or electricity. Apparently the generator had quit running during the night. After hurriedly dressing, Terry went down and checked the generator. It was full of gasoline and oil and the batteries were charged. So why wouldn't it run? Terry and the maintence crew tried everything to get the generator running but to no avail. So Terry called the generator repair company. However, the repairmen refused to come to make the repairs. They said they had never been paid for the generator in the first place and that the service contract had run out many months ago. Oh, Brother!

While Terry was trying to decide what to do next, a couple of the employees came and told him about another problem. The sewer pumps would not work and that meant that the sewer holding tanks could not be pumped out—and they were full. Evidently as the generator slowed to a stop, the voltage ran so low that the sewer pumps overheated and burnt up. We wouldn't be able to pump out the sewer from the houseboats or use our toilets. Now, pardon the pun, we were really in deep doo-doo!

Of course, Terry tried to get permission from our boss to get the repairs done but found out that he had gone to China for a month-long vacation. (Wonder where he got the money to do that?) We certainly could not wait for the repairs to be made until the boss got back from China. The NPS learned of our problems and told us to fix them or they would close the marina. Terry knew he could not let the marina close. So he took matters into his own hands. He persuaded the generator company to come to the marina and make the needed repairs. Then he ordered several porta-potties to be delivered. He knew it might take a few days to get the sewer pumps repaired, and we had to have toilet facilities. You see, those damaged pumps lay at the bottom of the sewer-holding tank with three thousand gallons of raw sewage on top of them. So to get to the pumps, Terry and the maintenance crew had to take the sewage out of the tank, bucket-by-bucket. Then the pumps were taken into town to be repaired. Even though the repairs were made as quickly as possible, we used the porta-potties for a week. What an experience that was. Terry paid for the pump repairs out of his own pocket knewing he would probably never be reimbursed. But it was worth it to he had kept the marina running. Soon everything was back to normal and we sent those porta-potties back.
P.S. Happy Birthday, Terry.

The marina passed another NPS inspection with excellent ratings. We could now boast a perfect rating for the entire year. We wished we could be as excited for the rating that UNI had received. It received its third marginal rating that year. Apparently, the accounting officers still had not submitted the required financial statement to the NPS. In fact, we were not sure any proper financial report had ever been submitted to the NPS. Also, UNI was in contractual violation for not having the sewer and water plants completed, approved and running. The NPS warned the Navajo Nation that unless they saw to it that the water plant and the sewer system were approved and in good running order, SJM would be closed on June 1st. Terry and I had done all that we could. It was now up to the Navajo Nation to see to it that UNI fulfilled its obligations. We knew the employees had learned all that we could teach them. They had the desire, the ability, the confidence and the technical knowledge to run the marina. Now they just needed the chance. If UNI and Mr. K would be honest and keep the monies available, the employees would see to it that the marina survived and prospered. Terry and I suspected that our days as the managers of SJM were rapidly coming to an end. We knew Mr. K was not happy with our constant communication with the NPS and the representatives of the Navajo Nation. But that was our job. We would not lie to anyone. The NPS and the Navajo Nation had asked questions regarding our problems at SJM, so they knew about the unpaid bills. Even the vendors themselves began making phone calls to the NPS. Many of them threatened to pull out their equipment such as the gas pumps, the generator and even the houseboats if they did not begin to receive payment toward their bills.

APRIL 18 – 24

This was the weekend for our first annual fishing tournament. Carl and Bart had taken a large board (five feet long and three feet high) and cut it into the shape of a fish so the customers could hang fish on it and take pictures of their trophies. We had hoped that this event would draw many customers to SJM and Lake Powell and add to our revenues. We advertised the tournament in the local newspapers and on local radio stations throughout the Four Corners area. Prizes were available to the winners, and a three-day houseboat trip would be given for the grand prize. But with several days of cold rain, the tournament turned out to be a bust. However, by the next weekend the fishing turned good and fish boils were plentiful. A fish boil occurred when larger fish (in this case, striped bass, also known as stripers) tried to eat or feed upon smaller fish (silver shad) that swam near the water's surface. The feeding frenzy caused the water to look like it churned and boiled with activity; thus the name, striper boil. It was an exciting thing to fish these striper boils. When a hook was tossed into it, with or without bait on the hook, the fisherman was always sure to get a fish. One afternoon, when business was very slow, Terry and several employees, including myself, got out fishing poles and fished the striper boils around the marina docks. We took out fifty to sixty striped bass that afternoon. The fish ranged in weight anywhere from five to ten pounds apiece. What fun we had, especially since it helped us escape from our recent marina problems. That evening we enjoyed a large and yummy fish fry. Now that isn't a fishy tale!

APRIL 25 – 30

We learned that three arrests were made in connection with the murders of the two Navajo policemen last December. One was one of our own employees: Bob. We were all in shock. Not our Bob! He was apprehended at work by the FBI and the Navajo police and taken into custody in handcuffs. Along with two other local Navajo boys, he was taken to Salt Lake City, tried by jury, convicted and sentenced to life in prison. Bob had worked with us since the opening of the marina. He was tall, about five feet ten inches, and very, very thin. He kept his black hair at shoulder length and he was the youngest of our employees: just eighteen. He worked on the docks and did general maintenance. He was always on time to work and never missed a day. Bob was especially quiet and shy. However, he wore a soft smile and was the first to volunteer for any job or task. We couldn't (and wouldn't) believe that Bob was capable of such a violent crime. It seemed impossible that we could have worked so closely, day by day, with someone who was considered to be a killer. Terry and I and all of the employees just knew there had to have been a set up made by the real killers who were probably drug dealers from another area.

Many strange things had eyebrows rising when it came to the rumors of drug deals that supposedly went on throughout the Monument Valley area. I, myself, had seen several questionable events. One afternoon while driving back to SJM, I came upon a small white jet plane parked on one of the gravel side roads that led to the marina. It was such a strange sight to see a jet parked in that isolated and desolate area that I hesitated and slowed the truck. When I saw two dark skinned men in white suits get out of the plane, holding machine guns, I sped on. Were these men drug dealers? I was not going to wait around and see. The employees told stories about seeing occasional parachute drops of small packages and, on moonlight nights we had heard small planes circle the area. But nobody would, talk about the suspected drug deals or the murders of last year. The real killers knew who they were, and they knew their secret would be safe. It was fear that kept mouths closed around Monument Valley. Sadly, Terry and I were never to see Bob again.

It was almost eighteen years later that we learned about Bob's fate. He had spent several years in prison before being paroled for good behavior. He had returned to his family and his home in Monument Valley to start a business and rebuild his life. He married and became a father, and it looked like the past would be put behind him. However, it wasn't meant to be as Bob was found one day, apparently murdered. To this day no one has been held accountable for his death. Also, years later, we were chatting with a fellow Navajo employee when we started speaking about our SJM days. He knew about the two Navajo policemen who had been murdered and knew that several drug dealers, not the two Navajo who had been convicted of the crimes, had murdered them. We had been right! Sadly, it was fear among the Navajo that had kept the truth hidden and is still hidden to this day.

CHAPTER TWELVE
May 1988
The Strike

MAY 1 – 17

Houseboat rentals for May looked great. We were renting twelve to fifteen boats every week. The kids were busy running the marina and seeing to the daily operations. They had the knowledge and all of the tools they needed to keep the marina going and were ready to take over the management if needed. It seemed that everything was going smoothly. However, there was a black cloud that loomed over the marina and a fateful storm was approaching. Terry and I could foresee it. SJM was slowly being suffocated and was struggling for its life.

Mr. K continued his battle against the NPS using underhand methods to cover up the inability or unwillingness to pay the bills. He also tried to keep the unpaid vendors at bay by making promises he knew he would not keep. Greed seemed to be his only motivation and the welfare of the marina and its employees did not appear to be important to him. He continued all of the financial restrictions he had placed upon SJM and even tried to make more. SJM was choking as if a large noose was tightening around its neck. But, in fact, the marina still had plenty of life if it would be allowed to live. Its spirit was strong but Mr. K was weakening it. We felt powerless. During its first year of life, the marina had survived many long and hard struggles. Every time a problem had come up, the employees fought and scratched until the problem was solved. But apparently Mr.

K was not going to cooperate within the NPS rules and guidelines. We feared that the future looked bleak for SJM and its employees.

MAY 18

A meeting was held among the NPS, Terry and me, men from the board of directors of UNI, Mr. K and his lawyer, Mr. Custer. It was ironic: the Sioux had a Custer against them and now the Navajo had their Custer, too.

The water and sewer issues were discussed at great length. The NPS asked what the status of the package plants were. Our boss said that the package plants had been approved. We knew they had not. The subject of the unpaid bills was discussed. Our boss said that the bills from the vendors had been paid. We knew they had not. At this point the NPS asked several men, who had been waiting outside of the meeting room, to join the meeting. Two of the men were from the company that built the package plants and they testified that indeed the package plants had not been approved. Next, two other men, who were some of the unpaid vendors, related that they had not been paid. Things were getting tense. Our boss's face was pale with anger. His eyes squinted and his lips tightened into a grimace. We could almost imagine steam coming from his ears. We kept silent; we didn't dare say a thing.

The NPS gave UNI and Mr. K a final warning. If the water and the sewer problems were not taken care of and if the bills were not paid within the next thirteen days, SJM would indeed be closed down on June 1st. The meeting was adjourned.

When Terry and I got back to the marina, Mr. K, Mr. Custer and one of the UNI directors were waiting for us. Mr. K said, "Did you tell the NPS about the unpaid bills?"

Terry replied, "Yes, when they asked us if those accusations were true, we said that they were. We would never lie to them or to you."

"You are fired," yelled Mr. K loudly as he struck the table he was sitting at with his fist.

Terry and I immediately went down to the marina to tell the employees what had happened. They were all wide eyed, and we could see they were completely bewildered. Why? What happened? They had certainly not expected this turn of events. Mr. Custer followed us into the office and cautioned us not to speak to the kids. Terry and I left the marina store and went to our home to calm down and collect ourselves. We were upset, to say the least, but not really surprised. We knew that Mr. K blamed us for all the troubles at SJM to disguise his own failures and bad decisions. He did not realize that by firing us he had put a nail in his own coffin. The NPS knew the truth. That was what really mattered.

That evening after the marina closed for the day, all of the employees came to our house. All twenty-two of them arrived at the same time. Some of them cried, some of them cursed and some just sat quietly. Everyone who talked, talked at once, some in English and some in Navajo. Their world at SJM had experienced a big jolt. I fixed hamburgers and French fries as everyone discussed the events of the day. What shall we do? Let's go on strike. We can't work without you. We aren't ready to run the marina on our own. Can we? These were some of the questions being asked.

Terry calmed everyone down and tried to answer all of the questions. "You are able to run the marina without us. We are very, very proud of you all. We have taught you everything you need to know about the marina," Terry told them.

"Do you want to leave us?" they asked.

"No, of course not, but if we have to leave, we leave with the confidence that you can do what you need to do. You must keep your marina open and running." We advised the employees that no matter what they did, they should first consult their spiritual elders, their parents and the Oljato community leaders. Also, when a final decision was made, they should all stick together. So everyone took off to ask advice from those who could help them cope with the important decisions that had to be made for SJM. This was not just about the two of us being fired. It was about the future of the employees and their families and the surrounding community's economic success. Terry and I sat alone and stared at each other. We felt anxious but pretty much emotionally drained. We wondered what would happen next.

MAY 19 – 22

Well, we didn't have long to wait. The next morning we looked out the kitchen window and saw all of the employees sitting in their vehicles waiting for the marina to open. They were all lined up in a long line about two blocks from the marina compound. What were they up to? Promptly at 8 a.m. they started their *chidi* (cars and trucks) and slowly drove to the marina store. They got out of their vehicles and formed a large circle around the boss who had come out to talk to them. We watched as a lengthy discussion ensued and continued for about an hour. Then all the employees got into their vehicles and drove away. What had happened? Who was going to work today at the marina? There was a knock at our door, and Bart came in. He told us that the employees had decided to go on strike. They had presented a list of demands to the boss and were now waiting for his decision. Here were their demands: first, they wanted Terry and me reinstated as the managers of SJM; second, they wanted Mr. K to quit; third, they wanted answers to where all the money from SJM had gone; fourth, they wanted the promotions and pay increases they had been promised; fifth, they wanted to be involved with all upper management decisions. And, lastly, they requested that the NPS be actively involved with the local Navajo chapter delegates to help confirm that the marina's upper management fulfilled their end of the concession contract. They wanted the marina to be a success. The employees decided to go on strike until their demands were met. So they did. They were prepared to go the distance.

A strike line was established where the Navajo Reservation met the National Park boundary, about one mile from the marina compound. The employees were sticking together, and they had the total support of their families and community leaders who also wanted answers as to why we were fired and what was going to happen to their children and their marina. Everyone in the Oljato area respected the strike and did not cross the picket line. When customers who had houseboats reserved to rent came up to the picket line, they stopped. The employees told them that the marina was still open, and they could go ahead and rent their houseboats without any trouble. But when the customers found out why the employees were striking, they honored the picket lines and did not cross, each and every one of them. Of course, this would hurt the marina's revenues and the customers would lose their deposits. The support the kids were receiving was amazing. They just wanted honest answers and the chance to keep their own marina running.

Terry and I left the house and drove over to Goulding's to make some phone calls and reserve a U-Haul trailer. We had been given five days to leave SJM. On the way back home, we stopped and sat with the kids at the picket line. We had coffee and chatted with them. Many of the local folks and parents of the employees had come to sit on the picket line to support the employees and to make sure their kids were safe. Not surprisingly, everyone was congenial and very calm. They had built several small campfires to sit beside, as the weather had cooled and evening approached. The kids were very determined.

As we sat among our friends, the Sheriff of San Juan County pulled up to the picket line in his squad car. He motioned Terry and me over to his car. "Are you two all right? We heard you were being held hostage by the SJM employees," he inquired with an official look on his face.

Terry exclaimed, "What?"

I laughed out loud. "Are you kidding?" I asked. "We are just fine."

Terry said with a grin on his face. "These kids would never hurt us or anyone else, for that matter. This is not another Wounded Knee!" He was referring to an Indian extremist group who, in the 1960's, caused havoc by holding a strike against the federal government on an Indian reservation in South Dakota. During the strike, force was used and it became bloody, with some people getting killed. It caused a media frenzy and there was trouble for years over unresolved issues. Its memory still lingered, and no-one wanted a repeat.

"Well, I came to protect you and help in any way I can," the sheriff said.

"It's the boss and his cronies we need protection from," Terry replied. "Could you escort us into the marina store so we could get our personal belongings? We haven't had a chance to do that yet."

So the sheriff went with us and stood inside the marina store. We went into the office and Terry and I picked up our personal effects. Mr. K and his lawyer chided us verbally but we did not respond in any way. We quickly and quietly left. The sheriff never had to come to the marina again.

The next morning Terry went to pick up the U-Haul, and I began to pack our belongings. We had talked with the NPS after we were fired and they were furious with Mr. K. They knew we did not deserve to be fired, but they wanted the Navajo Nation and UNI to try to solve their internal problems by themselves. The NPS asked us to come to Page and remain there until the situation at the marina cooled down. They said they wanted us to be available in case our testimonies were needed, or they needed help in understanding what had happened at SJM. They also knew that the employees would listen to us, and we might be needed to help defuse the strike. This was the first Native American strike that any NPS concession had ever experienced, and there were few guidelines for the NPS to know how to proceed with the situation.

MAY 23

The day came to leave the marina. Terry stepped outside of our mobile home and saw Jim Fatt standing beside the U-Haul. Terry greeted him with a Navajo good morning.

"Just where do you think you are going?" Jim replied, in English. We had spent one year at SJM and did not know Jim could speak English because we had always used a Navajo interpreter when we communicated with him. The joke was on us! He and Terry embraced each other and laughed. We sat for a while with him and his wife, Jean, discussing the previous two days' events. It was going to be hard to leave these wonderful people and our kids.

"Come on honey. It is time to go". Terry gently touched my arm. Looking into his caring brown eyes, I slowly nodded. Yes, I knew it was time. He was trying to be brave but I knew he shared my sadness. Our hearts ached and we knew we would miss this place and our friends. Would our paths cross again? We were proud of the accomplishments that had been made here in this isolated and remote part of the world. Nothing compared to the deep respect and regard we felt for these people whom we had come to know and love. They had become our family.

Saying goodbye has always made me unhappy, but this time it was soul-destroying. The kids stood in a circle around us, their faces downcast, and no one spoke. We had stuck together through many physical hardships. As one large family we had shared many emotions: fear, courage, hope, anger, sorrow, competition, teamwork, satisfaction and, yes, even some disappointments. We celebrated life through new births and suffered a shock when murder occurred. We had developed love, honor and harmony between us. No one could bear to look at each other because no one wanted to show weakness with tears. We slowly embraced each other, one at a time, and clasped hands in farewell. Still not a word was uttered.

As we tried to start our motor home's engine, it stalled as if to say, "No don't go." But we did have to leave. As we drove down the old Navajo trail that first brought us to SJM, we heard loud shouts of *Hágoónee' shık'ıs dóó Ahéhee'*, Goodbye friends, thank you. I began to cry.

Had it really only been twelve short months since we first traveled down this same road? As I recalled the events of the previous year, I realized that they all seemed to be linked to this old trail. The road began to take on a living personality of its own. Who had first made this path? Were their spirits kept alive through the traditions practiced by the Navajo here?

As I looked out of the window of the motor home, I gazed at the desert landscape that had become such a part of us. I had traveled this road almost every day for the last year, but I felt as if I was seeing it for the first time. The sky was the brilliant blue seen in the feathers of a blue jay. The red sandstone formations in Monument Valley rose in the distance and looked like sentinels guarding our little marina. The cloudless sky gave all the surrounding mesas depth and grandeur. How could we leave what had become a home to us? Small delicate yellow and white flowers lined the red sandy road. Bursts of red and orange blossoms were jumping out from behind an occasional green bush. The sagebrush, which was scattered everywhere was alive with deep purple blossoms. Yucca cactus looked like tall candles standing with their long green pointed leaves and their white blossoms stretching toward the sky. It was truly a beautiful sight, and it held a wonderful treasure that we had been so fortunate to be a part, San Juan Marina. I began to feel a little better about leaving and I prayed that we would see our friends again soon.

MAY 24 – 31

We drove the motor home to Page and settled into the KOA Campground. We rented an RV site for two weeks and waited to see what would happen next. The NPS communicated with us through Pamela and she let us know how events were proceeding at the marina. We wished we could have helped our kids fight for their cause but knew that we had to stay out of it. If, by some miracle, we were asked to return to the marina, we would. We had little hope of that if UNI remained as the sub-concessionaire. The Navajo Nation had to live up to the contractual agreements between it and the NPS, and that had nothing to do with us. We experienced many emotions during those two weeks. We felt sad and yet happy and proud. We felt hopeful but knew the reality of the situation would not find us employed at SJM again. We felt guilty for leaving the kids but knew they had the grit needed to fight for their cause. We felt unwanted and frustrated, but also we felt loved by the kids and encouraged for their success. Now we had to pull ourselves together and plan for our own future. After all we had been fired from our jobs, and we knew our money would hold out just so long and go just so far. Our emotions had to be corralled and decisions had to be made as to where we should go and what we would do next.

The past year had been a physical challenge and an emotional rollercoaster for us. We had submerged ourselves into the duties at SJM and had not thought of what we would do or where we would go after SJM. Now those choices had presented themselves sooner than we had envisioned. It was hard to think about that future when we still worried about our beloved kids and their marina. We wanted only what was best for them. We did, however, feel a little rejected. Didn't anyone care what was happening to us? We understood why the NPS didn't want to involve us since we had left SJM. They wanted the Navajo Nation to solve its own problems. They knew we had done everything humanly possible to keep the marina running. We also knew the kids had to take charge of their own destiny at SJM. So we waited.

Meanwhile, back at the marina, even though all of their demands had not been met, the employees were working again. Terry and I would not be rehired. They unhappily accepted this fact but were glad that the strike was over. The employees knew they could manage and run their marina, but they were still wary of their future. Promises had been broken before. There were still many issues to be resolved. The NPS was also glad to have the marina open. Revenues were needed to keep the marina running and media coverage was causing bad publicity. The marina was still the best place for customers to get gasoline and supplies needed to access the San Juan River arm of Lake Powell. Houseboaters came back to SJM, and the rafting companies returned. The customers were enjoying themselves and spending their money. However, they were not aware of the struggles that the employees were involved with to keep the marina running. The bills were still not being paid, and the water and sewer problems continued. Thirteen days had passed since the NPS had warned of the closure of SJM.

JUNE 1

As promised the NPS closed SJM today. They were not waiting any longer for compliance on requests that the problems be corrected. The water and sewer plants at the marina site had not been approved, so they were deemed unsafe to operate. Bills had not been paid. UNI, under the oversight of the Navajo Nation, had been given ample time to comply but had made no effort to correct the situation. The closing of the marina caused major inconveniences to the customers, the NPS and the employees and their families. And the saddest thing was it all could have been avoided.

Members of UNI, Mr. K, representatives from the Navajo Nation and even the chairman of the Navajo Nation, rushed to the NPS regional office in Denver, Colorado, to plead their case. An immediate compromise was needed to keep SJM afloat and the joint concession contract intact. After many long meetings, the Navajo Nation evidently was able to convince the NPS that all contractual requirements would be met as soon as possible. So on June 6, 1988, SJM was reopened on a temporary and limited basis. The NPS would certainly closely monitor the new promises made by the Navajo Nation and UNI. Maybe there was still hope for the marina and its employees.

On June 1, the same day the marina was closed, we left Page for our hometown in central Illinois. Since leaving SJM, Terry and I had not received any notification that our involvement in the affairs of SJM were needed or wanted. We decided that it was best if we got on with our lives. We decided to spend the rest of the summer months with our families and friends, healing our wounds and planning for our future. We agreed that we would do some traveling around the country in our motor home and look at different areas where we might want to live and work. We would let fate and destiny decide where we would start our next adventure. It had been almost one year to the day that we had first arrived at SJM.

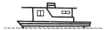

CHAPTER THIRTEEN
June 1988 – January 1996
Now The Truth
Is Revealed

JUNE – NOVEMBER 10,1988

As the summer came and went and fall approached, many changes were seen at SJM. We were keeping in touch with our friends via phone calls and letters, as we wanted to keep abreast of the progress of SJM and the future of our friends. The marina was kept open for business, but almost all of the original employees were replaced. We heard that the management had said that the new employees would be 'more loyal and less bothersome' since they were brought in from outside of the Oljato area. Of course, they did not have the loyalties to the success of SJM that our kids had, and they did not know the history of the struggles that we had endured. We were sure that the new employees did not know or have experience in marina operations. Several new marina managers (most of whom also had no marina experience) were hired and fired, all without proper notification and approval from the NPS. The water and sewer systems were still not safe nor were they operational. Bills were still unpaid. Communication between UNI and the NPS was virtually nonexistent. UNI kept complaining about how the NPS was causing all of their problems. In truth, the NPS was being very patient. By letting the marina remain open and giving the management time to clean up their act, the NPS hoped to keep the twenty-year contract with the Navajo Nation solvent. Apparently the Navajo Nation and UNI did not get the big picture. By losing the contract at SJM, all other future proposed marina contracts on Lake Powell with the Navajo Nation could be jeopardized.

NOVEMBER 11, 1988

The headlines in the local newspapers read: "National Park Service Suspends Concession Contract at San Juan Marina." It was now official. SJM was permanently closed. UNI and the Navajo Nation were cited for repeatedly failing to meet state and federal health standards for the water and sewer systems at SJM. They were also cited for violation of twelve additional issues in the concession contract including the unpaid bills. This was indeed a very serious turn of events. Instructions were given to customers to rent houseboats on Lake Powell at other marinas or apply for rental refunds. What a shame! With the closing of SJM, there would be no gasoline for the customers and no place for the river rafters to rely on. Neither the NPS nor the Navajo Nation could predict if or when the marina would be open for business again. What would happen to our struggling marina and the ones who cared so much for it? A heavy cloud of sadness hung over our hearts, and we knew that our friends were feeling that sadness, too.

NOVEMBER 21, 1988

Apparently the Navajo Nation and the NPS did work out a compromise so that SJM could remain open on a limited basis. According to the NPS records and the local newspaper articles, UNI began working on getting the approval on the water and sewer plants and tried to get all of the other violation issues resolved.

JUNE 4, 1989

Another seven months passed before SJM finally reopened. Apparently the approval to safely operate the water

152

and sewer plants had been received from the proper state and federal authorities. A sewer lagoon had been built to solve the environmental concerns about pollution. Supposedly the labor problems were solved. A ceremony for SJM's reopening was being planned for June 21, 1989. We don't know why, but that ceremony was postponed too.

AUGUST 19, 1989

The newspapers reported the tragedy. "A violent and sudden flash flood, caused by isolated severe thunderstorms raced through Paiute Farms Wash near the Oljato area and headed toward San Juan Marina. It was 10:45 p.m. The swift raging waters rolled over and through the marina with fierce purpose. The marina dock structures were ripped from their anchors. Several boats were capsized and carried downstream. Other boats were simply missing. Damages occurred to the gasoline and water facilities that made repairs impossible. Reconstruction costs for San Juan Marina were estimated in the thousands of dollars. Fortunately there were no injuries to any person or persons."

So it had ended. SJM would not be rebuilt. The local Navajo said that Mother Nature was so worn out from all the struggles of her friends that she decided to take matters into her own hands. The Blessing ceremony that had been held in the beginning days of SJM only worked as long as those who cared and looked after it were walking in harmony with their friends and surroundings. Unfortunately, that had ceased long ago.

The NPS officially closed SJM and removed all of the remaining structures. Customers would not come anymore. Except for a few broken pieces of concrete from the floor of the marina store, nothing remained. One could not tell SJM had ever existed. But it had existed and had been a very important and meaningful part of so many wonderful lives. That is why we have told this story: to remember and honor it and the people who loved it and fought for it.

It is very important for the reader to know this: each and every employee from SJM went on to achieve many accomplishments in his or her lives. They did not give up just because they could not work at the marina. None of them ever went on welfare or went without jobs during the years that followed. We, as well as they, are especially proud of this accomplishment. Maybe in small way we gave them the example they needed to keep their pride and hope high through any adversity. But no matter what we gave to them, it was little in comparison to what they gave to us.

So what happened next?

August 20,1990 – December 1996

From 1990 through 1995, the Governor of Utah, at the request of the local Navajo who had been interested in the welfare of SJM, launched a major and thorough audit into the affairs of UNI. The investigation eventually involved many other Navajo governmental agencies and people. The investigation even led to the Navajo chairman who was in office at the time.

What the audit revealed was astonishing. The misuse of the monies from SJM by UNI was just part of a larger fraud. The audit showed that over twelve million dollars in a space of fifteen years (before and during the existence of SJM) had been funneled by UNI into several people's personal pockets. The money never got to the local Navajo who needed it. They had been promised these funds and had worked to develop economic success in their communities, as an example, SJM. Indictments were passed to at least a dozen people. Eventually the federal government got involved and the Navajo chairman was convicted of fraud against his own people. The Navajo government had been fashioned after our Anglo government. This was good. But, evidently they also learned how to run a government and line their pockets with cash. Sound familiar?

All the time we were working at SJM, we instinctively knew that there was a major problem in how UNI and Mr. K were running things, but we could have never imagined what was actually going on. Would or could we have done anything if we had known? Somehow, after finding out about the results of the audit and what had happened, we felt vindicated. We knew we had done everything in our power to make the marina a success. Neither our employees nor we had any part in the fraud. We knew the events of the marina's failure were not our fault. It never occurred to us that we were up against such evil and overwhelming odds. The marina's purpose was good and promising. The hearts of its employees were honest and pure and hopeful. We had all survived and were the better for it. Now the truth would set us free.

CHAPTER FOURTEEN
January 1996 – June 19, 2004
The Circle Is Completed

Terry and I did not return to Monument Valley for many years. We continued to work and manage other marinas and resorts all along the Colorado River system. We lived on Lake Mohave in Nevada, Lake Amistad in Del Rio, Texas, and in January 2002 we moved to the Grand Canyon. The adventure at the marina was a subject that we talked about regularly, and the faces of our kids were always present in our minds. The memories of SJM were happy ones for us, but we also felt sad and incomplete. Whenever we tried to read the personal diary we had kept while at the marina, our hearts ached so much that we rarely finished it. We wanted some closure to our pain. We also wanted to know that our efforts had not been in vain and that our kids had forgiven us for leaving them. Their Christmas cards and letters never mentioned the marina.

One night I had a very realistic dream. I was among the Ancient Ones in Navajoland. I sat among many elders around a ceremonial fire listening to drums and flutes. The chanting of the medicine men grew louder and louder. I felt as if I were being called to participate in some prcdcstined path and was being honored for accepting the calling. An overwhelming feeling of peace, purpose and excitement fell over me and continued with me as I woke up from my dream. Immediately upon rousing myself to full wakefulness I knew what I had to do. I picked up my diary and began to read it. Then I picked up my pen and began to write. It was time to tell the SJM story. My purpose was clear. It was important the record be set straight, it would be an opportunity to heal our hearts and it was time to honor the kids and the memory of SJM.

It wasn't until we began to research the newspapers to find out what had happened during the years after our leaving, that we learned of the state and federal audit. It was a shock but also a relief that the kids had been strong enough to pursue the truth about the way SJM had been handled. Now we longed to see our kids again and celebrate the truth with them. However, it would be another six years before Terry and I were able to return to Monument Valley for a visit. Over the years we had kept in touch with our kids through yearly Christmas cards and notes. Every note or card mentioned how much we were missed and details of children born and jobs held. But the subject of the marina was never discussed. It was becoming more and more important for us to see and embrace our kids again and revisit the SJM site where we still felt so connected.

In the spring of 2003, almost fifteen years to the day that we had left SJM and said good-bye to our kids, we returned to Monument Valley. Wanting to surprise our friends, we did not give any advanced notice of our visit. Would they recognize us? We had grown older, our bodies had become more round and our hair had shades of silver in it now. Would they even want to see us again? How many of our kids still lived in the Monument Valley area we were not sure. As we stopped the car and went into the restaurant at the old Goulding's Trading Post, we felt as nervous as we had when we arrived at the marina so long ago. The first of our kids that we saw were Bart and Kathy. We were instantly recognized. Shouts of surprise, long embraces and tears of joy between the four of us filled the room. We had not been forgotten. Before long the word spread and several other of our kids were in our arms. Mary Ann and Abe, Iris, Sally, Dale, and John welcomed us with warmness.

Even Jim and Jean Fatt, who were driving by in their pickup truck, recognized us and stopped to welcome us back. It was a wonderful reunion. It felt as if we were finally coming home. There was only one more thing to do. It was time to go out to the old site of SJM and face our feelings.

As we drove down the old road, which had only changed slightly by time and weather, we became nervous with excitement and dread. Memories flooded back as we passed familiar landmarks. Finally we were there. Everything was different but somehow familiar. It was a strange feeling. Confusion and sadness wrinkled our brows. There were many questions going round and round in our heads as we tried to comprehend what had happened here so long ago. Even though most of its physical appearance had changed, we could still envision where the marina and all the buildings had been. Where there was once blue water, now thick green groves of tamarisk bushes grew. Where the little wooden marina store had stood, only bare ground remained. As we kicked the earth trying to find any little remnant of our life there, we found several little pieces of the concrete floor that had been painted blue. Somehow it was a comfort. We drove up where our mobile home had sat. We could see the remains of some of the white gravel that had been our driveways and how they had been arranged in a circle.

The storm and the flash flood that followed had washed away a lot of the earth around the marina store and had left only a small part of the peninsula where the docks had once been anchored. But as we looked across the large gully that once was our marina bay, in our minds we could still see all of our houseboats tied to the neatly kept wooden docks. The marina launch ramp had originally escaped most of the flood damage. With no water at its edge, it seemed out of place. Even the San Juan River had taken a new course since the flood. Originally the river had run along the west side of the canyon flowing into the waters of Lake Powell. Now the San Juan River flowed near where the marina had been on the east side of the canyon. We walked upon what would have been the old shoreline, down to where a new waterfall was in the making. The old river still carried tons of silt with it and the water's force could be loudly heard. The local folks had named the new attraction, Fatt Falls.

Gradually we began to feel a sense of relief and calm about seeing the marina site. We came to realize that even though the marina had ended in such a violent way, eventually, the incoming force of the silt of the San Juan River would have brought it to this same conclusion. So would the dropping lake levels, due to drought. We recalled the prediction by the NPS that the river would have eventually filled the marina's bay with silt in a few years anyway. That was why SJM was only a temporary site. It had never occurred to us that the silt would have actually filled the bay, or that it would have eventually looked like it did now even if the flood had not occurred. There was no lake there any more, just a snaking river with a waterfall. Well, that was that. Now we looked forward to catching up with our friends.

While living at SJM we had been interested in having a traditional Navajo wedding ceremony. It was a way to demonstrate our acceptance of the Navajo's belief in *Hózhó*: the harmony one has with one's self, with others and with one's surroundings. But in those days the Navajo *Hataałı* would not perform such a ceremony for any non-Navajo. We never forgot about our desire and apparently neither did our kids. The first thing they wanted to do for us was to plan a wedding. "Our *Hataałı* will do it for you now," they said. Needless to say, we were very excited. There are very few Anglos who are invited and allowed to participate in a traditional Navajo wedding ceremony performed by a Navajo *Hataałı*.

Terry and I had been given honorary membership into the Navajo Edgewater Clan while living at San Juan Marina. But to be properly married in the Navajo way, the bride and groom could not be members of the same clan. So we would have to be adopted into separate clans. I chose the *Ashįįhi Dóone'é* (the Salt Clan) of Jim Fatt and Terry chose the *Tłízíłání Dóone'é* (the Many Goats Clan) of Dale. An emissary, our long-time Navajo friend, Pamela, was chosen to go to the Medicine Man and make sure that this special request could be carried out. Enthusiastic approval was given, and now the groom was to ask for the bride's hand in marriage.

Terry and I accompanied Pamela to the hogan of my new Uncle Jim and Aunt Jean. They lived down the old road that Terry and I had first traveled on to work at SJM. Uncle Jim was away herding his sheep and goats and Aunt Jean sat in the doorway of the cool shade house cording virgin wool that had recently been hand sheared from her own sheep. She gently and quickly pulled pieces of wool from a bag with one hand and added it to the wool spindle that she kept moving rapidly in her lap with her other hand. She did not stop as we spoke. Since there was an old Navajo taboo that cautioned eye contact between the groom and his mother-in-law, Terry and Aunt Jean did not look at each other. I went and stood beside Aunt Jean with my hands folded in front of my skirt. Pamela nodded at Terry. This was his cue to proceed. Nervously and with hesitation (I knew he wanted everything to be done as properly as possible) he asked, "Aunt Jean, may I have your niece's hand in marriage?"

Smiling but never stopping her spinning or lifting her head, she nodded and whispered, "*Aoo'*," Yes.

Terry said, "*Ahéhee',*" Thank You.

I bent down and gently gave Aunt Jean a hug. Now we could start planning the wedding.

Traditionally, at this point, the dowry would be negotiated. In the old days, the groom's family would offer as many as twelve horses, ten cows, several sheep as well as a lot of turquoise jewelry, or whatever it took to secure the bride. As a token of tradition, even though we were not officially adopted, Terry gave Aunt Jean a five-dollar bill as a deposit toward my dowry. Because of this, I became known as "the five-dollar-down-deposit bride." Everyone got a big giggle out of this. In addition, the Navajo believe it is not polite to discuss money matters in public, so we are not at liberty to discuss the financial arrangements of my dowry.

The date of the wedding was chosen and the location decided upon. Terry's new clan brother, Dale, had built a large, traditional hogan and a new shade house near his home in Oljato. He graciously offered its use to us for the wedding ceremony and the feast/reception afterward. Only very special Navajo ceremonies and special events were held in this hogan. Needless to say, we felt very privileged and honored to be invited to have our wedding there. Uncle Jim consented to preside as the Medicine Man over our ceremony. He instructed us, through family interpreters, on how a traditional Navajo wedding was conducted and what our participation would consist of. We were taking this very seriously and reverently.

The sun rose into a crystal blue, cloudless sky on the morning of June 19, 2004. We had just celebrated our thirty-fifth Anglo wedding anniversary, and this day would be our Navajo wedding day. When we awoke, Pamela was already headed out to the shade house to help with getting the wedding feast ready. There were fires to build, fresh-butchered mutton to cut up and grill and lots of fry bread to make. Dale and his wife, Elizabeth, our hosts, were already busy making the necessary preparations to welcome the guests. Terry and I arrived about 9 a.m. Terry and Dale ran errands, and I helped cut up the mutton. Many of the women of our new families were arriving, and we all kept busy preparing the food. There was a home-like atmosphere, and it was peaceful there in the shade house. A gentle breeze blew through the recently cut tree branches on the roof of the shade house and the fresh, clean, fragrant smell of sage and pinyon was in the air. Everyone spoke softly and almost reverently, some in Navajo and some in English, as the work continued to completion. I felt serene and happy. Once again, it seemed as if time had stopped. I wanted it to fill my soul and last forever. It felt safe and it felt right.

Finally, it was time for Terry and me to dress for our wedding. As the guests continued to arrive and make their greetings to each other, Terry and I put on our traditional Navajo wedding clothes that a Navajo seamstress had made for us. I wore a dark sage green, gathered, three-tiered, floor-length skirt and a pale sage green, long sleeved, buttoned-down-the-front blouse. A deep red coral, thirty-strand necklace, with earrings to match, graced my bodice. Two turquoise and silver bracelets were worn, one on each wrist. My new clan sister, Sally, presented me with a handmade brooch that she had made. It is about three inches high and consisted of two small Navajo moccasins with leggings attached, placed on top of a small white doily. Tiny red flowers sprang up from the top. I wore it on my blouse's collar. I attached a faux hairpiece tied in the middle with white yarn to the back of my head to simulate the traditional Navajo hairstyle of a double bun.

Terry's outfit consisted of a cowboy-styled long-sleeved shirt and pants. The dark forest green shirt hung over his white Levi jeans with a headband to match his shirt. Several blue turquoise and silver necklaces hung around his neck, and large turquoise and silver bracelets were snug on his wrists. A concho belt made of silver squares with large chunks of turquoise on them went around his waist. We both wore authentic Navajo leather moccasins made of brown cowhide that tied at the sides. They are very comfortable.

The only thing left to add to my wedding attire was the customary traditional Navajo sash belt. This item is only worn for special occasions and worn only by special people. Pamela insisted that I borrow and wear her sash belt, and I gratefully accepted. It was made of dark red, white and dark green yarn that had been tightly woven into geometric patterns It was about five to six inches wide but four or five feet long and could be wound around the waist several times. Strands of fringe hung at each end of the belt. There was a certain way the sash belt had to be worn, so my attendants worked together and tied it around my waist. They cinched it up tightly like a corset. This helps the posture but not one's breathing. We all laughed hysterically when the girls tried to get the belt as tight as they could, and I began to gasp for air as my face turned blue.

A very special gift of two Navajo blankets in brightly stripped colors of red, green, yellow and orange were given to us to complete our wedding costumes. I was shown how to drape mine around my shoulders, and Terry carried his over one shoulder. We both presented a very striking, colorful, and impressive site. We felt very special indeed.

Meanwhile Aunt Jean was making our blue corn mush wedding cake that was to be used in the wedding ceremony. Traditionally the mother-in-law always prepares it. The ingredients and the way it is made are held in secret. When it was finished, the mush cake was put into a newly hand made Navajo basket with the wedding design woven into it. The consistency of the mush cake, after it has set for a while in the wedding basket, forecasts the outcome of the marriage. To have a successful marriage, the cake must be thick, not runny. Our cake turned out perfectly. Now it was time for the bride to go into the hogan where the groom was waiting. His friends and family had already taken their places to the north of the hogan's entrance or to the left of the groom.

Uncle Jim led the bridal procession from the shade house toward the hogan. He carried the water-filled wedding vase in one hand and his medicine bag filled with corn pollen in the other. I followed him carrying the wedding basket being very careful not to juggle or shift the cake inside. I placed the wedding basket in front of Terry, making sure that its position was in alignment with the hogan's entrance, the east. It was important the basket not move from this position to ensure the success of the marriage. It is believed that many marriages are not long lasting if the basket is moved around during the ceremony. The bride's family and friends took their places to the south of the entrance or to the right of the bride. Terry and I sat down together facing the east. We looked at each other, clasped each other's hands and gently smiled.

Uncle Jim took the water vase and instructed us how to proceed. He handed me the vase and I poured water over Terry's cupped hands. He washed his hands and I poured some more. This was done four times. Then Terry repeated what I had done, pouring the water over my hands four times. This was to show our recognition of the seriousness of our actions, our intent to continue our lives together and the cleansing of our hearts toward each other. The number four has special meaning to the Navajo.

Next, Uncle Jim took corn pollen from his medicine bag and sprinkled it on the corn mush cake. He prayed softly in Navajo as he made a circle around the edge of the cake and crossed it in the center. He then instructed us how to partake of the cake. Terry took the first bite by dipping two fingers into the mush and eating from them. Next I took a bite in the same manner. We then helped ourselves to more cake, taking it in turns, starting at the east where the basket design opens and continuing from all four directions and then from the center. After we had taken the first required bites, the wedding guests were all invited to come forward and partake of our wedding cake. This part of the ceremony symbolized the harmony and support between Terry and me and our new extended families. Terry and I finished off the rest of the cake licking our fingers until they were clean. The mush was very tasty.

Continuing with the ceremony, our dear longtime friend and marina mentor, Jerry Sampson (whom we fondly call Papa Sampson,) read a special prayer that honored God and His creation. After being married thirty-five years, this prayer represented our continued commitment toward each other and the harmony of our lives together. Here is a copy of that prayer:

God in heaven above please protect us and
the ones we love.
We honor all your creation as we pledge
our hearts and lives together.
We honor Mother Earth and ask for our
marriage to continue to be abundant and
grow stronger through the seasons.
We honor fire...and ask that the commitment
of our union be warm and glowing with love
in our hearts.
We honor wind....and ask that we sail
through our future journeys safe and calm.
We honor water...to sooth our marriage that
it may never thirst for love.
We pray for harmony and happiness, as we
forever grow young together.

Uncle Jim then gave his blessing to our marriage. Among the many private wishes he gave us he added, "You are now a part of our family and we are a part of yours. You will never be lonely or want for friendship. You are always welcomed in our home, on our land and among our families."

In the traditional Navajo wedding, the bride and groom do not receive gifts. They give them. This act shows responsibility and acceptance of the duties that are now expected of the newly married couple toward their families and their extended clan members. This act also reinforces being a part of a larger family unit and culture. There were, however, a few traditional gifts given to special guests and family members at this point in the wedding ceremony. Terry and I had two Pendleton blankets to present to certain special family members. The blankets were wool, white in color and had tan and rust traditional Indian markings on them. The one with the plain-banded edge (called the Chief's blanket,) Terry gave to our host, Dale. The other blanket with the fringe (called the bridal shawl) I gave to Aunt Jean. As a part of the bride's dowry and as a thank you gift, we gave Uncle Jim a large silver and turquoise bow guard for his wrist. When he opened his leather wrapped package and saw his gift, he smiled from ear to ear. We knew he was very pleased. He shook our outstretched hands, and we could feel his sincere pride and thanks.

At this point in the ceremony, Terry and I exchanged personal gifts to each other. Terry gave me a silver and gold wedding band with a Navajo story on it. I gave Terry a silver money clip with a Navajo dance depicted on it. Now it was time to formally thank all of the guests for their attendance and support and invite them to the shade house to partake of the wedding feast. Terry and I stood outside the hogan's only door and hugged and thanked everyone as they came out. The warm regard that we felt from everyone enclosed us like a cocoon. It was a peacefully happy and joyous contentment that we experienced. Together, hand in hand, Terry and I left the hogan and strolled toward the shade house. We now understood and felt the distinct awareness of how it felt to walk in the Path of Beauty in Harmony.

Terry and I joined the line at the shade house where the reception feast was being held. There was plenty to eat and everyone piled their paper plates high with food. The air was filled with the odor of mutton grilled over pinyon and juniper wood. Hot mutton stew containing fresh carrots, celery and potatoes simmered next to the blue corn soup on the outdoor stove. Fresh lettuce salads, coleslaw and baked beans added variety to the feast. Fresh fry bread was plentiful. I had even helped make some of it myself. Everyone ate heartily as they socialized among themselves. For dessert, I served up the several flat sheet cakes I had made. They were made of white cake and decorated with white icing. Red and black Kokopellii figures were stenciled on the tops of them. (Kokopelli figures represent fun, happiness and laughter.) Everyone thought they were yummy and it wasn't long before they were all gone.

Later that afternoon most of the guests had departed for their homes after saying their goodbyes and giving best wishes to Terry and me. They took all the leftovers they could carry, as this was also a traditional custom of sharing. The early evening sun began casting long shadows across the nearby mesas and their rocks began to hold purple hues. Terry and I sat with Uncle Jim and Aunt Jean and a few close family members enjoying their companionship. We chuckled as we watched a white baby goat wander about, jumping and playing around the shade house. Several small children were trying to catch the little fellow, and these antics provided at least an hour's worth of entertainment. Someone put some wild apricots on the open fire to cook, and soon we were enjoying them, too. We talked about many things as we sat together. We remembered San Juan Marina and how we had first met each other. We recalled the hard struggles and the many, many accomplishments that had been made at the marina. We laughed happily at some of the memories, and we were saddened by others. We caught up on what had happened to each of us during the last fifteen years, and we spoke of our future together. We all agreed that the story of San Juan Marina was a good story and needed to be told. The honest account of what had happened to us all at San Juan Marina would stand as a testimony to all who had lived and benefited by its presence. The story would be a living memorial to all of those employees and their families who gave their all and asked for nothing but hope in return. Fate had brought us together and we had taken our place in the history of this people and their land. It had been an important adventure, and we would tell the story to all we knew.

Terry and I departed from our new family as the sun finally set behind the black silhouetted mesas in Monument Valley. It had been a good day. We would be seeing our friends again, and no matter where our adventures would take us, we would never be far from our new family. The circle of our Navajo connection was now complete.

NAVAJO FRYBREAD
Dah di niil ghaazh

Mix together:
  2 cups flour
  1/2 tsp. salt
  2 tsp. baking powder
  (some Navajo also use 1/2 cup dry powered milk, but it isn't really needed)
  warm water (enough to form dough into a ball, about 1 cup).

Knead the dough with flour until it is soft but not sticky. Let it stand for two hours.

Get a large skillet and put approximately ½ inch of melted lard (or shortening) into it. Let the lard get very hot.

Break off plum-sized pieces of dough and begin to flatten with your hands until it forms a flat disc about the size of a saucer (or if you can do it, the size of a plate).

Drop into the hot skillet and fry on one side until golden brown and puffy. Then turn over and fry until done. This only takes a few minutes.

Terry Edwin Eilts

For more than thirty-eight years, Terry has been my spouse, partner, friend, lover, soul mate, companion, co-worker and sidekick in many memorable and exciting adventures in our journey through life. His adventurous spirit and need to always seek new encounters, in his work and play, is what led us to San Juan marina. His patience, good nature and a strong desire for achievement made the trip successful. His energy and my need for ongoing change have made and continue to make our wanderings fun and unforgettable.

Even though Terry has given me the honor of being the author of Floating Hogans, it is "our" story.

Thank you, Terry.